RELIGION AND FREEDOM
IN THE
MODERN WORLD

HERBERT J. MULLER

RELIGION
AND FREEDOM
IN THE
MODERN WORLD

CHICAGO & LONDON

THE UNIVERSITY OF CHICAGO PRESS

Library of Congress Catalog Card Number: 63-20911

THE UNIVERSITY OF CHICAGO PRESS, CHICAGO & LONDON
The University of Toronto Press, Toronto 5, Canada

ACKNOWLEDGMENTS

IN BOTH humility and pride, I am pleased to record my deep gratitude to the Frank L. Weil Institute for Studies in Religion and the Humanities, which honored me by its invitation to deliver the series of public lectures that compose this book. I must hope that I have not abused the freedom permitted by its breadth of interest in religion and culture, or religion as a humanistic study.

It is also a pleasure to express my gratitude to the Cincinnati Friends of the Institute, and to the staff of Hebrew Union College, for their most genial hospitality during the course of the lectures.

CONTENTS

Introduction

1

CHAPTER I

Religion and Revolution

6

CHAPTER II

Christianity, Culture, and Morals

24

CHAPTER III

Religious Revolutionaries: Kierkegaard and Dostoevski

46

CHAPTER IV

Religion in America

67

CHAPTER V

The Religious Revival

89

CHAPTER VI

The Challenge of the World Crisis

110

vii

INTRODUCTION

Since this book is an outgrowth of my History of Freedom, two volumes of which have appeared, I feel obliged to restate once more the premises on which I have been operating. By freedom I mean "the condition of being able to choose and to carry out purposes." This involves both the primary dictionary meaning of freedom *from* external constraint and the more positive idea of freedom *to* do as one wishes, or real opportunities as well as rights. An unemployed illiterate, for example, may be subject to no more legal constraint than his fellow citizens, but he enjoys less real freedom than a prosperous educated man. The study of freedom so defined accordingly embraces familiar kinds of freedom—political, intellectual, religious—but also related ideals of social justice, such as the rights of working people, and it calls for attention to culture as well as government. In this view the Western democracies deserve the name of "free societies" that they are pleased to give themselves. Despite all their shortcomings they certainly are freer in most respects than were the historic societies of the East, or than are the assorted dictatorships and Communist-controlled nations today.

As for religion, I am treating it primarily as a historian and am dealing only with its social consequences, specifically its relation to issues of freedom in the modern world. I therefore waive the metaphysical question of its truth, and touch only incidentally on other matters of vital concern to theologians, as to ordinary believers. Thus when Paul Tillich raised the question "Can religion be used as a tool for something else?" he said that the answer was, "of course," no: religion is ultimate; it cannot be the tool for anything non-ultimate. To a historian the answer is obviously yes: religion always has been used for worldly purposes, especially political purposes, in ways that Tillich himself has emphasized because of his concern with the ultimate. He also specified some natural consequences of the religious spirit that are of particular concern in my study—religious conservatism, authoritarianism, intolerance, and transcendentalism. In any case, emphasis on the social utility of religion is especially characteristic of modern thought, including the popular writings of churchmen.

These point to another distinction, necessarily rough but highly important, which is often overlooked in discussion of the meanings and values of religion. On earth, in history, one has to deal with three broad levels of religion: the highest spiritual level, represented by the teaching of the great founders, prophets, and holy men; organized religion, represented by established churches with vested worldly interests; and popular religion, representing how the faith works out in the thought, feeling, and behavior of ordinary men. Organized religion, always a necessary mediating agency, is the easiest for a historian to deal with, since the doings of the churches are written all over the record. I assume, however, that he cannot ignore the pervasive influence of the lofty spiritual ideals, difficult though it is to assay, or the equally difficult questions raised by the fruits of popular religion. Together these help to explain why modern America, say, may not look much like a Christian society, but still looks quite different from Hindu and Moslem societies.

In short, my limited subject is nevertheless a very large and complex one. It is no less so because I confine myself primarily to Christianity, for the simple reason that this is the dominant religion of the Western world, which in turn has dominated modern history. Historic Christianity has embraced remarkably diverse, conflicting tendencies, and may therefore be called the most catholic, the most dynamic, the most ambiguous, or the most inconsistent of the higher religions. Regarding the issues that concern me, some thinkers today view Christianity as the very fountainhead of the Western tradition of freedom, others as the major historic enemy of the cause of freedom. As I see it, the truth lies somewhere between these extremes, but not in a comfortable middle ground. On the basis of its heritage from Judaism, and then from Greco-Roman culture, Christianity did more to promote the growth of freedom than did any other of the higher religions, as the historic record of the great Eastern societies plainly suggests; while it also opposed freedom of thought, speech, and conscience more fiercely than did any other religion except Mohammedanism, which shared its tradition as the most militant, exclusive, and intolerant of the world's religions. During the period I am covering here, roughly from 1800 to the present, in a society grown notoriously secular, it has played a less influential but still an ambiguous role. Among other things, the churches have tended to support the growth of some secular interests (such as capitalism) while continuing to attack secularism on principle or from habit.

At every point, accordingly, I am faced with the problem of selection and emphasis, among mixed, shifting tendencies that can never be measured or weighed; and I can never be certain that my judgments are sound and fair. One who tries to study the social consequences of religion will soon discover how little we really *know* about its effects on behavior. Since my primary concern is freedom, I can be sure only of giving some offense to the devout—especially in the opening chapters, where I dwell on the prolonged tendency of organized religion to oppose the movements toward popular government, civil liberties, and social reform. I must therefore beg the reader to bear with me to the end, by which time I hope to have presented a fairly comprehensive, decently balanced account. In this humble spirit I should add that while I have naturally attempted a dispassionate, objective study, befitting a historian, I cannot pretend to be wholly impartial. I am not neutral on the basic issues of freedom, but essentially am committed to the stand of John Stuart Mill: "The only freedom which deserves the name, is that of pursuing our own good in our own way, so long as we do not attempt to deprive others of theirs, or impede their efforts to obtain it." On the other hand, I am not committed to any positive religious belief, in particular about the good that God-fearing men should pursue; but my possible advantage in detachment may be offset by want of inside understanding or by insufficient concern with the ultimate. At any rate, let it be understood that whether or not God approves the free society, my subject here remains the relations of Christianity to this kind of society in the revolutionary modern world, and that in my view these relations are basically ambiguous. I do not apologize for failing to arrive at any pat conclusions.

A word, lastly, about what is commonly called "spiritual freedom." This is essentially a psychological or subjective freedom, involving the feeling of security that may result from simple faith, the more positive feeling of liberation that may come with intense religious experience, and so on. It seems to me an important kind of freedom, necessary for a historian to take into consideration, even though most social scientists prefer to disregard it because it is subjective and strictly unobservable; for states of mind are very real, they plainly influence the ability to choose and carry out purposes, and as plainly they have real social consequences. Nevertheless, such spiritual freedom is not to my mind the very essence of freedom, neither is it the distinctive essence of Christianity, and least of all is it the hallmark of free societies; for it can be enjoyed by slaves, it has been enjoyed in all kinds of societies, and free societies are historically distinctive because they have established more objective, specifiable kinds of freedom. I prefer to call it "peace of mind," if only because of the common tendency to identify "true" freedom with wisdom, virtue, holiness, and other spiritual goods. Then I should emphasize that the conditions of life in a free society by no means guarantee such peace of mind, any more than they do goodness or happiness. The freedom to pursue our own good in our own way implies the constant possibility of lazy, stupid, evil, or fatal choices.

⋆ I ⋆

RELIGION AND REVOLUTION

Fɪʀsᴛ ᴀɴᴅ ʟᴀsᴛ, it should be emphasized that religion was far from being a major inspiration of the political, industrial, and intellectual revolutions that have so profoundly transformed modern civilization. Much more apparent are the changes that these revolutions have effected in religion. The Christian churches continued to play an active part in this worldly history, to be sure, and as surely Christian idealism was a factor in the struggles for democracy and social justice, but throughout the nineteenth century the major churches were most conspicuously conservative when not reactionary forces, just as established churches have always tended to be. Simply because they by now generally support the cause of a free society, I feel obliged to begin with the tedious story of their long hostility to this cause—a familiar story that may no longer be really familiar enough. Only in this view can we appreciate the significant changes that have come over the churches in our century, and the current role of religion in a free society. Moreover, this tiresome past is not dead and done with; its legacy is still very much alive, in the attitudes alike of many churchmen, many workers, and many critics of the churches, and in the continued conflict between secular and religious interests. Let me cite the authority of an eminent spokesman of Christianity today, Paul Tillich. "The first word," he has said, "to be spoken by religion to the people of our time must be a word spoken against religion."[1] Or in traditional Catholic terms, let us say that it is necessary to call in the devil's advocate.

Such remarks may seem gratuitous to many Americans because of their unique history, which calls for a separate chapter; but here the American Revolution may serve to introduce the basic ambiguities that we need to keep in mind as we review the hostilities in the nineteenth century. Beginning with an appeal to "the laws of Nature and Nature's God," the Declaration of Independence asserted the "self-evident" truth that all men had been created equal, with inalienable rights to life, liberty, and the pursuit of happiness. Thereby it restated the essential principles of equality, brotherhood, and the dignity of the person that are proclaimed clearly enough in the Bible, and that heretics and rebels in Europe had kept appealing to since early in the Middle Ages. At the same time, the many American loyalists who opposed the Revolution were by traditional standards just as good Christians, if anything better ones, than the rebels. The self-evident truths rehearsed in the Declaration of Independence had not been at all evident to the leaders of Christendom for some seventeen centuries, at least in any literal sense, for any practical political purposes; almost uniformly the leaders had supported an aristocratic society under monarchical government, in which common men were denied equal rights or any

[1] *The Protestant Era*, p. 185, in the Phoenix Books abridged edition (Chicago: University of Chicago Press, 1957). I shall not hereafter annotate quotations, since this book is designed for general readers and is not primarily a research work. I make an exception here because the short chapter, "The Word of Religion," from which I quote, seems to me an especially admirable introduction to the subject.

voice in their government. The authors of the Bible never referred to "the laws of nature"; the idea of natural law as a universal principle of justice had come out of Greek philosophy, and then been embodied in Roman law. Thomas Jefferson, author of the Declaration, was echoing the common belief of his century, the Age of Enlightenment, that Newtonian science had confirmed this principle; no devout Christian, he revered a different authority—in his own words, the "great Trinity" of Bacon, Newton, and Locke. Religion was not in fact an issue or clearly a vital factor in the American Revolution, which was primarily a secular affair. The founding fathers carefully refrained from mentioning God in the American Constitution. John Adams wrote: "It will never be pretended that the men who set up the American governments had interviews with the gods, or were in any degree under the inspiration of Heaven."

Thereafter Americans generally did so pretend. Most came to believe that their novel democracy was a truly Christian commonwealth, blessed by God; and to some incalculable extent their religious faith bolstered their faith in themselves and their national ideals. But meanwhile the French had stirred much more alarm among political and religious conservatives when they made a revolution in the name of the same inalienable rights of man, or of liberty, equality, and fraternity. Although the French Revolution was not started by godless men, it encountered strong opposition from the Church in France, whose bishops were allied with the nobility and bent on preserving special privileges such as American churchmen did not enjoy. As a powerful state church it had also incurred much hostility during the Age of Enlightenment. When the early moderate leaders of the revolution lost control of it, such hostility became much more pronounced; under the Jacobins Christianity was officially superseded by cults of Reason, the Fatherland, or at best a nameless Supreme Being. Hence the revolution frightened the ruling classes all over Europe as a threat to the entire traditional order, political, social, and religious. Edmund Burke in particular won his lasting fame as a political philosopher by his attack on the basic principles of popular government, which he said menaced the very foundations of European civilization—"the spirit of religion" and "the spirit of a gentleman."

Christianity responded to the challenge with evident success. The Napoleonic wars were attended by a marked religious revival, of which the epochal Romantic movement was among other confusing things one symptom. After Waterloo the Roman Catholic church regained much prestige on the Continent, and with it political power; the papacy proceeded to tighten its organization, to reassert and maintain its authority in both temporal and spiritual matters. Protestantism gained less conspicuously at first only because it had suffered less from the revolution; it was due to become so vigorous and expansive that Kenneth Latourette's scholarly history of religion in the nineteenth century is almost wholly optimistic.[2] He emphasizes that the growing strength of Protestantism was more remarkable because it had to contend with not only the growing skepticism due to science but the disruptions of the Industrial Revolution, which was concentrated in Protestant countries, and which steadily drew men from the naturally pious village into the rootless, restless, worldly city. Latourette also emphasizes the ever more active and extensive participation of Protestantism in the missionary movement, which in this century spread the Christian

[2] *Christianity in a Revolutionary Age*, Vol. I: *The Nineteenth Century in Europe: The Protestant and Eastern Churches* (New York: Harper, 1959).

faith all over the world. In general, it might appear that the French Revolution proved salutary for Christianity.

Yet "the spirit of religion" to which Burke appealed was not clearly purified by this ordeal, and certainly it was not liberalized. In the reactionary era following Waterloo, the major churches everywhere supported Prince Metternich's policy of restoring all the traditional powers of monarchs and the nobility, or "gentlemen," and his relentless warfare on all popular agitation for more liberty and equality. One symbol of the era was the famous Holy Alliance dreamed up by Czar Alexander of Russia, in which the monarchs of Prussia and Austria joined him in solemnly proclaiming their resolution "to take for their sole guide the precepts of that Holy Religion, namely, the precepts of Justice, Christian Charity, and Peace." Metternich himself privately called this a piece of pious nonsense, while the monarchs soon gave liberals good reason for their belief that Holy Religion was only dressing up an alliance designed to preserve despotism.

In the literary world Chateaubriand set the fashion with his immensely popular *Genius of Christianity* (1803), which celebrated especially the genius of Roman Catholicism. The German Romantics, such as Novalis and Schlegel, typically became apostles of authoritarianism in both church and state. In England, Wordsworth and Coleridge kept clear of Rome, but indicated plainly that the spirit of religion still tended to be ultraconservative in social and political matters. France itself produced the most vigorous spokesman of the reaction in Joseph de Maistre, who recently has had something of a vogue again. In attacking the entire faith of the Age of Enlightenment—in science, in freedom of thought and press, in progress—de Maistre attacked "the intellectuals" as a class, proclaiming the theme of anti-intellectualism that resounds to our day. Conservatives are still fond of quoting his ridicule of such abstractions as Man, the alleged creature endowed with Rights: "I have seen Frenchmen, Italians, Russians, but as for Man, I declare I never met him in my life." Skeptics might remark that the Holy Ghost gave him no trouble, though presumably he had never met it either; but in any case he showed as little love of men. While he maintained that war was literally "divine," he deplored the humanitarian concern over the earthly lot of common men, in effect regarding "fraternity" as only another revolutionary abstraction, like the more dangerous "liberty" and "equality." He pined for the good old days of the Inquisition, which his church in fact made some effort to restore.

De Maistre's bitter war on the ideals of the French Revolution testified, however, that they had survived the revolution's apparent failure, which Metternich also recognized. The power of these ideals became more obvious in the wave of popular revolutions in 1830. The Roman Catholic church met this challenge just as it had dealt with the Protestant Reformation, by an absolute refusal to compromise. The papacy rejected the whole democratic creed, while calling more insistently for the complete obedience of all Catholics to its decrees. Pope Gregory XVI denounced the "deadly and execrable liberty" of the press, and with it "the absurd and erroneous maxim, or rather insanity" of liberty of conscience. Pius IX entered upon the longest pontificate in history (1846–78) by displaying some mild liberal tendencies, but he was soon frightened out of these by another wave of revolutions in 1848; and thereafter he fought against the popular cause with unflagging energy and invective. He summed up his opposition to modern civilization as a whole in his celebrated *Syllabus of Errors*, a list of eighty heresies, in which he condemned every article of the liberal, progressive faith. In 1870 Pius crowned his work by putting through the dogma of papal infallibility (though unfortunately just two months before the new kingdom of Italy ended the Papal State, reducing the spiritual leader of mankind to a "prisoner of the Vatican"). This dogma alienated some Catholic rulers and many prominent laymen, such as Lord Acton, who wrote an article exposing how it had been railroaded through the Vatican Council; but it was clearly acceptable to most of the clergy. Likewise the papal denunciation of the liberal heresy was indorsed by eminent Catholics, above all by Cardinal Newman, one of the leading religious spokesmen of the century.

The papacy then began taking a more liberal stand under the long pontificate of Leo XIII, the much more moderate successor of Pius IX. He came to believe that the Church might get along as well with democracy as with other forms of government, and specifically advised French Catholics to stop warring on their republic. In his famous encyclical *Libertas* (1888) he described liberty as a noble gift suited to the dignity of reasonable beings. In effect, however, he confined reasonableness to the Catholic faith. Liberty of worship he qualified by the proviso that men should never be permitted the license of false worship; freedom of speech and press must not mean the toleration of "errors," or "diseases of the mind"; liberty of education must always be tempered by the realization that only truth makes us free, so that no education is really free unless it is in accord with Church teaching. Leo also wrote that "the Church usually acquiesces in certain modern liberties" only because of expediency "in the extraordinary condition of these times"—"she would in happier times exercise her own liberty." Similarly, he maintained medieval principle by declaring the superiority of the Church over the civil power, categorically denying the state independence in religious matters: "It is not lawful for the State to hold in equal favor different kinds of religions."

The basic issues raised by the Church's stand, in a world that kept moving toward the free society anyway, are best illustrated by the plight of Lord Acton, who was at once an ardent liberal and a devout Catholic. One evident reason why he never wrote the History of Freedom to which he devoted most of his life (and which has been called the greatest book that was never written) was his difficulty in reconciling his dual allegiances.[3] He wanted to believe that Christianity was the main source of freedom, and that progress in freedom was the main theme of human history, or God's plan for man; but he was a thoroughly scrupulous historian, always respectful of the evidence, unable to gloss over the historic record of Christianity. He could not help recognizing plainer sources of freedom: in ancient Greece, then in the rise of science, secular rationalism, freethinking—against the opposition of his church. In his own day his belief in progress was included in the modern "heresies" denounced by Pius IX, and was attacked as well by his good friend Cardinal Newman. Upon the cardinal's death he worried again, in some 2,000 notes, over his basic dilemma; for Newman was a great and influential Catholic but not at all a liberal, rather an uncompromising enemy of his liberal faith, in favor even of persecution. To make matters worse, Acton saw freedom of conscience

[3] I might add that I have gone through the materials Lord Acton collected for this work—some 25,000 note cards. Even apart from the thousands of notes in which he worried over the unfortunate doings of medieval and Renaissance popes, they become rather pathetic, for they involve a great deal of repetition and include a great many quotations—copied in a meticulous hand—from books in his own library. For a long time he was apparently trying to maintain the illusion of progress on a work he must have known he would never write.

as the very essence of freedom, which in his well-known definition he summed up as "the assurance that every man shall be protected in doing what he believes to be his duty against the influence of authority and majorities, custom and opinion." Cardinal Newman flatly denied any such "right of private judgment," just as the Church has always denied freedom of conscience, on principle.

At any rate, the practical consequences of the Church's stand are still with us. While it succeeded in maintaining the allegiance or the obedience of the Catholic world at large, it confirmed the antagonism of non-Catholics, which persists in the widespread suspicion of the Catholic church today. It also stirred up considerable opposition in its own realms, which likewise persists; anticlericalism has typically been most bitter in Catholic countries, where it was aggravated by struggles over the control of public education. It was bitterest of all in France, the greatest Catholic country. Here the clergy maintained a powerful bloc of opposition to republicanism long after the French Revolution, consistently supporting the interests of monarchy. At the end of the century, under the Third Republic, animosities came to a boil in the ugly, portentous "Dreyfus affair." As disagreement over the sentencing of Captain Dreyfus broadened into a violent controversy over the national interests and the basic principles of all modern society, the French Church and its faithful followers ignored the advice of Pope Leo to support the republic; they lined up solidly with the ultraconservative monarchists, and were as solidly supported by the Catholic press all over the world. The affair was uglier because churchmen (especially the Jesuits) joined the monarchists in exploiting anti-Semitism to win popular support; they linked the alleged guilt of Dreyfus (the only Jewish officer on the

French general staff) with the sins of the "Jewish" republic and the machinations of "international Jewry." By thus inflaming the prejudice that had been erupting in Germany, Austria, and Russia, they also increased the hostility of intellectuals to the Church, and assured it both a political and spiritual disaster when the innocence of Dreyfus was conclusively proved. And if by now few but intellectuals remember an affair that one may hope will in time be dead and done with, in this pious spirit I think it important to remember that anti-Semitism is no recent aberration, but deeply rooted in Christian tradition. Neither the Catholic church nor the Lutheran church in Germany took the lead in denouncing Hitler's persecution of the Jews, which could indeed have been justified by some of Martin Luther's tirades against them.

The political record of Protestantism in the last century was characteristically much more mixed, given its innumerable different sects. Its basic principles of individualism and of "protest" against any human authority claiming absolute right were naturally more conducive to the growth of a free society; it kept breeding dissenters, nonconformists, rebels. It was in fact the dominant religion in all the major countries except France that made the most marked advance toward democracy, in time identifying itself with the gospel of progress. Yet its major churches did not lead this advance. Rather, they tended chiefly to resist it. The most powerful of them were state churches, and these were in general the most stubborn defenders of the old order.

In England the Anglican church was in the vanguard of the violent Tory reaction against democratic ideals that dominated politics in the Napoleonic and post-Waterloo era. The Archbishop of Canterbury expressed its temper by helping to defeat a bill providing for elementary schools; Protestant as well as Catholic churchmen were long fearful of public education as a threat to the traditional order. The Anglican clergy opposed more solidly than any other class the mild Reform Bill of 1832, which made the first step toward democracy by somewhat extending the suffrage, and then opposed as vehemently the Chartist movement in the working class, which had been left without a vote. Thereafter the Anglican church was less intransigent than the Roman church, permitting more latitude to its unorthodox members, but at best it only accommodated itself to the political changes that went on despite its leaders. The Methodist church, the largest of the "nonconformist" churches in England, was in this respect little more disposed to nonconformity; its leaders mostly went on the record as political conservatives. On the Continent, German Lutheranism, which constituted the largest and most influential Protestant church, differed chiefly in its quiescence. It kept more aloof from political life, or in effect maintained a more placid alliance with the Prussian monarchy. In his enthusiastic account of nineteenth-century Protestantism, Kenneth Latourette could say only that "Germany did not completely lack" Christians of a progressive spirit in a revolutionary age. Paul Tillich, himself a Lutheran, observed less cheerfully that the Lutheran churches remained indifferent even when Hitler came into power—until he began interfering with their own affairs.

Possibly more fateful was the attitude of the Protestant churches toward the movement for social reform. This grew out of the humanitarian movement that got under way in the eighteenth century and was given added impetus because of the Industrial Revolution: immediately the shocking conditions of women and child workers in factories and mines, then the growth of industrial slums—a concentrated poverty and squalor that were more glaring because of the marked gains in collective wealth and power. On this subject Latourette again writes enthusiastically about the contributions of Protestantism, pointing out that it was much more active than Catholicism, for example in the crusade against slavery. But it turns out that social reform was due chiefly to the "Christian spirit" of some laymen; he acknowledges that most high churchmen remained indifferent when not positively opposed to their efforts. And granted that the Christian spirit was a real force, the whole humanitarian movement remained primarily a secular movement, aided by the spread of democratic ideals that high churchmen also opposed.[4] It recalls that there had been no such concerted efforts to improve the earthly lot of serfs and workers in the medieval "Age of Faith," or under the Protestant Reformation either; the agitation began in the secular Age of Enlightenment. As Dean Inge confessed, "It is disquieting for Christians to have to admit that the growth of humanity, in the sense of humaneness, does not owe much to the Churches."

Now, in fairness to the churches I should observe that their apparent callousness was due not simply to a deficiency in Christian spirit, but to more complex feelings. Many churchmen felt that they should on principle keep aloof from social and political problems, confine themselves to the purely spiritual or the ultimate; the devout may still feel that otherwise the Christian gospel may be reduced to mere matters of social utility. Others who felt concern took for granted that they

---

[4] As an incidental example, the Royal Society for the Prevention of Cruelty to Animals was organized in England by a clergyman in 1824. The Society for the Prevention of Cruelty to Children was not organized until sixty years later, and then by a layman.

should work only on the hearts of men, as preachers had worked ever since the prophets of Israel and Jesus himself. One plain reason why Jesus neglected to spell out the democratic implications of his teaching is that he was by no means a political reformer, seeking to change laws and institutions; and we still hear often enough that new laws do no good unless the hearts of men are purified. Many other clergymen, moreover, believed like the earnest Hannah More that the poor—the poor who will always be with us—would be both more virtuous and more content if they accepted their poverty and their lowly status. In particular, society's responsibility for poverty or misery was obscured by the "Protestant ethic," the sturdy gospel of individual responsibility: worldly success, like salvation in the life to come, was wholly up to the individual, aided only by the grace of God.

Nevertheless, social reformers had legitimate complaints about the attitude of the churches, even apart from the many clerics who were simply complacent in their own security. However high-minded, aloofness from social problems amounted to a false neutrality, an acquiescence in apparent social injustice or oppression of the poor. The Protestant fondness for crusading against sin or vice, such as the evils of drinking and gambling, only emphasized the common failure to get at the root causes. Working on the hearts of men was evidently no more effectual than it had been all through Christian history, during which peasants and workers had been oppressed, but it was still less promising in a society that was glorifying competition, free private enterprise, and the profit motive, or what once upon a time was called greed. The Protestant gospel of individualism, always liable to obvious abuse, was as obviously corrupted by the many conservative churchmen who supported the ruling class, now a business class devoted to a gospel of economic individualism and to the sanctity, above all, of private property. Most leaders of the major churches upheld this sanctity even though it involved the rights of a corporate kind of property that was quite impersonal, and though God himself (judging by Scripture) never dreamed of United States Steel. Likewise most were hostile to the labor union movement. Some even managed a Christian justification of the gospel of wealth; in America Bishop William Lawrence won a dubious fame by proclaiming that "Godliness is in league with riches." In defending this gospel—easing rich camels through the eye of the needle—the bishop dwelt on an idea that Protestantism had helped to make popular: the poor—whose plight had aroused the passionate indignation of the prophets of Israel, and who had been blessed by Jesus—were now known as "the idle, shiftless poor," or as "the masses," the chief menace to both godly virtue and civil order. Another popular religious theme was echoed by a Catholic archbishop of Baltimore (James Roosevelt Bayley): poverty was "the most efficient means of practicing some of the most necessary Christian virtues, of charity and alms-giving on the part of the rich, and patience and resignation to His holy will on the part of the poor."

The plain effect of the stand of the Christian churches, at any rate, was to alienate the working class, and to aid the rise of revolutionary socialism. St. Simon's effort to Christianize socialism made little headway. Robert Owen, the first major reformer produced by the Industrial Revolution, flatly repudiated the Christian churches; when he evolved his co-operative, socialistic program he proclaimed it as a new religion, "the most glorious the world has seen, THE RELIGION OF CHARITY, UNCONNECTED WITH FAITH." Karl Marx went on to attack all religion as the opium of the masses. His most influential brand of socialism stiffened the opposition of churchmen, who came to regard all socialism as inherently atheistic; but its appeal was a by-product of their conservatism. Workers were not repelled by the materialism of the Marxist philosophy, since they were compelled to be materialistic in their daily lives, having to think constantly of bread, on which their spiritual betters told them that man could not live alone. If most of them still considered themselves Christians, they felt that their churches were not on their side; socialists had more apparent concern for the dignity of the person than did most clergymen and pew-holders. The chief gain reported by Latourette in this respect is that the laboring classes in time became less hostile to Christianity: "By the end of the century they were indifferent rather than antagonistic."

The changes that the churches have undergone in our own century may therefore seem belated, but at least we may now better appreciate their significance. Under Pope Leo XIII the Roman church was among the first officially to proclaim the need for industrial reform. In another famous encyclical, Rerum Novarum (1891), Leo called for Catholic labor unions and legislation to protect factory workers. Catholicism has never really favored economic individualism, and in recent times the papacy has made clear that its opposition to communism does not imply an indorsement of unregulated capitalism. Likewise it has followed the policy of Leo by giving up consistent opposition to democratic government. In France the clergy are no longer hostile to the Republic, and most Catholics have come around to supporting it as loyally as men of other faiths or no religious faith. In all the democracies, especially the United States, Catholic attitudes if not avowed beliefs have been transformed by general acceptance of the ways of free societies. Most subscribe to the modern "errors" denounced by the *Syllabus* of Pius IX. In America they disagree, too, with Leo XIII's pronouncement that it is unlawful for a state to show equal favor to different religions.

Many Protestant churchmen have gone further, tending to a more active support of social reform as well as civil liberties. In the United States some have been so outspoken as to earn the honor of attack by the John Birch Society and other foes of the un-American ideas expressed in the Bill of Rights. The Anglican church has produced a "red" Dean of Canterbury. Lutheranism in Germany was ruffled by a religious-socialist movement, among whose founders was Paul Tillich. In general, churchmen everywhere have been realizing that the cry for social justice resounds in their Scriptures. Hence it is now a commonplace that there was much of the Hebraic prophet in the godless Karl Marx, whose moral indignation was hardly consistent with his allegedly scientific theory of economic determinism. When in 1937 the Oxford Conference took up the question of socialism and communism, and their relation to the prospective World Council of Churches, it approved a statement that God might speak to the churches more clearly through their enemies than through the churches themselves.

Yet this also recalls us to the disagreeable reality of the historic record of the churches, the reasons why God has had to speak through their enemies. Tillich laments that Christianity has not yet won the proletariat; in Europe especially, proletarian movements are wholly secular, prone to a radicalism unguided, as unblessed, by religion, because religion "has consecrated the bourgeois ideal" of property, while condemning socialism as materialistic. Catholic labor unions are much less strong than the Communists in France and Italy. Nor is the Church yet popular with champions of the free society. Most Catholic thinkers still ring variations on the theme that "true freedom" is only freedom to believe and do what is "right and good"—by Catholic standards; or as Bishop Fulton Sheen put it, "Tolerance does not apply to truth or principles." In Europe, prominent Catholics have continued to uphold the royalist, antirepublican tradition. The papacy has not committed itself to an explicit preference for democracy or shown a consistent concern for freedom except when Catholics as such are threatened; thus it did not oppose fascism in Italy, instead hailing Mussolini as "a man sent by Divine Providence" because he signed a concordat securing papal privileges. Most Catholic countries are at best shaky, unfledged democracies and remain susceptible to dictatorships, which in Spain and Portugal have been supported by the Church.

Today the struggle against communism accentuates a global problem in which organized religion is implicated, and which unhappily weakens the humane assumption that with better understanding always comes more good will. We often hear that the moral and political corruption of our time is due to the decay of religious faith—an issue I shall take up in the next chapter. Here I should remark that political corruption has for centuries been routine in countries where religion remains strong, notably in Catholic Latin America, in southeast Asia, and in the whole Moslem world. Beneath all the customary graft lay the deeper corruption of a rotten social system, in which the extreme wealth of a few was accentuated by the wretched poverty of the masses. The problem of combating the spread of communism is aggravated above all by the persistence of this flagrant inequality, which over the centuries the churches of these countries not only acquiesced in but helped to maintain; generally they supported the ruling class, offering only spiritual consolations to the wretched masses.[5] The aid we are giving to these poor countries still fattens mostly the corrupt and the rich, who stubbornly resist any basic social reform, refusing even to pay high income taxes. (One obvious reason why the Communist party is so strong in Italy, in spite of papal threats of excommunication, is that the many Italian millionaires vanish on income tax returns.) With better understanding of Latin American countries, Americans might be less disposed to pour millions down such venerable sinks. At least they should understand why Castro has been more popular in Latin America than we.

For such reasons political and religious conservatives may be dismayed, as Edmund Burke was in the French Revolution, because the spirit of godless revolutionaries remains typically much more fervent than the spirit of most Christians. The conspicuous exceptions of late have been such sects as Jehovah's Witnesses, which I think it fair to say are not conspicuously enlightened or lofty in spirituality. Since my main theme is by no means so simple as it may have appeared in this introductory chapter, I shall conclude on an ambiguous note. From studies made of the record of prisoners in Nazi concentration camps, and later of prisoners in China and Korea, it appears that those who stood up best under torture and brainwashing were Jehovah's Witnesses. Others who made a sturdy showing were priests, Communists, and criminals. It is often said that Americans need more faith; but even so I judge that any old faith will not do for the preservation of a free society.

[5] It should be noted that in the United States, too, churches that appealed to the "disinherited," such as the Negroes, have mostly tended to withdrawal rather than radicalism, likewise stressing the consolations of an afterlife.

∻ II ∻

CHRISTIANITY, CULTURE, AND MORALS

G OD IS DEAD," Nietzsche announced in the last century. Today the many leaders of the religious revival assure us that God is very much alive; yet they often declare what the revival itself suggests, that for most modern men God is indeed dead. And there is no question that the growth of a free society had much to do with his alleged decease. In the Age of Enlightenment some freethinkers began attacking him openly, establishing the tradition of disbelief that came down through Nietzsche. Others retained the Creator only as a social or philosophical convenience, reducing him to an absentee landlord of his creation. Thus Voltaire, who thought God was needed to make "the rabble" behave, remarked coolly that if he did not exist it would be necessary to invent him; and one might suspect that Voltaire had the feeling that has been attributed to Spinoza: "Between you and me, God, you don't really exist." Still more unseemly was the fate of deity among the unthinking, in thriving countries ever more devoted to material progress. God was not slain—he simply withered away, starved on an anemic formal respect lacking both love and fear. By now many nominal Christians believe that faith does not even require the formality of attending church. A living God might not bless America even though one public opinion poll indicated, rather surprisingly, that up to 90 per cent of Christian Americans were still inclined to believe in a literal hell; for it also indicated, less surprisingly, that of these some 90 per cent did not consider seriously the possibility that they themselves might go there. Presumably hell is where the bad Russians go; though one may doubt that Satan is really alive either.

Now, the most obvious reason for the alleged death of God is the notoriously secular culture of the democracies. To realize how secular it has become, one has only to look back to the Middle Ages, when Christianity was the main source of education, the basis of all philosophy, the subject of almost all major art, the frame for most serious thought about man, society, and the world; whereas the great bulk of modern art and thought has nothing to do with religion. As T. S. Eliot has lamented, a stranger from another society would never guess from most modern literature that ours was supposedly a Christian society. Like many other thinkers, Eliot maintains that religion has always been the vital core of culture, essentially identical with it; so he naturally concludes that our culture has been deteriorating. But purely secular thinkers have become as alarmed about the state of democratic culture, for reasons anticipated by Thomas Jefferson long ago when he expressed the hope that the human mind would recover the freedom it had enjoyed in ancient Greece. "This country," he wrote, "which has given to the world the example of physical liberty, owes to it that of moral emancipation also, for as yet it is but nominal with us. The inquisition of public opinion overwhelms in practice the freedom asserted by the laws in theory." Culture is a vital concern for political thinkers, too, because it molds the character and mentality of legally free men, the basic sentiments and habits of thought underlying the institutions of a free society, and its higher forms—the arts, sciences, humanities—are essential means to full self-realization, the assumed end of freedom.

In any case, freedom to choose and carry out purposes forces the question of ends, or of freedom for what. Since religion has traditionally declared the meaning and purpose of man's life, many writers assert that we have especial need of it today to combat the evident ills of our free society: the gross materialism and hypocrisy, the half-heartedness and hollowness, the lack of a clear national purpose, the lack of any high end. Most of us, I take it, might at least agree that a concern for spiritual values is essential to social health.

For this reason, however, we need first to discount somewhat the familiar complaints about our godless world. To begin with, Christianity has always been a live influence. Apart from the many deeply religious writers and thinkers, it has always been in the background of Western culture, just as it has always pervaded public opinion. Its influence is still apparent in the very opposition it has bred; T. S. Eliot also noted that "Only a Christian culture could have produced a Voltaire or a Nietzsche," while others might add a Karl Marx—a type hardly imaginable in historic India or China. Even so, such opposition has by no means destroyed the prestige of the churches in the Western world, which despite—or possibly because of—a fall in attendance seem more popular now than they were in Voltaire's day. All along there have been religious revivals, anticipating the recent one. Popular culture has never failed to accord Christianity at least a conventional respect. In America especially, public opinion permits no attack on religion; no candidate for high office today would dare to be as openly hostile to organized religion as Thomas Jefferson was. Recent sociological studies have shown that religion has considerable influence on popular belief and behavior, much more than was assumed by the positivists and determinists who long dominated the social sciences.[1]

In sizing up the state of culture, moreover, we need a broad concept of "spiritual values," centered on the spirit in man that seeks truth, beauty, goodness, and sometimes holiness. So considered, the spiritual includes the specifically religious but is not necessarily identical with it. Thus the brilliant culture of classical Greece was essentially humanistic, unique precisely in that religion was not so clearly its vital core as it had been in early oriental cultures; the Greeks alone declared a conscious faith in man's own powers of mind, which helps to explain why they were also the first people to declare a conscious ideal of freedom. In Western civilization this ideal likewise flourished with the growth of humanism and naturalism, of a concern with the values of life on earth. If secularism is a sign of deterioration, our culture has been deteriorating steadily for over five centuries; art and literature began achieving autonomy in the Renaissance, philosophy and science in the seventeenth century. Nevertheless, the secular works of Montaigne, Shakespeare, Rembrandt, Molière, Newton, Voltaire, Kant, Goethe, Beethoven, and innumerable others (including Jefferson) would seem to be a reputable cultural achievement. In the nineteenth century the secular spirit grew more obviously materialistic, often positively irreligious; yet this century still produced a great deal of remarkable work in all fields of culture, to which Americans and Russians began to

---

[1] I have in mind such studies as Gerhard Lenski's *The Religious Factor* (New York: Doubleday, 1961), which brought out basic differences in attitude in Protestant, Catholic, and Jewish communities—differences that are due most obviously to social class, but also to religious tradition, and that appear to be growing sharper rather than weaker. Politicians, of course, have long taken for granted that these differences count for a good deal.

contribute. At worst, "decadent" is not clearly the word for an era that displayed such unflagging energy and creativity. One who respects the human spirit cannot afford simply to sneer at the growing preoccupation with material well-being, for this involved much effort to improve the lot of common men; and wretchedness does not naturally induce a pure or lofty spirituality.

Such reservations, at any rate, recall my main concern. Granted that Christianity continued to exert a pervasive influence on Western culture, how wholesome, invigorating, and uplifting was this influence? Did it make for the "moral emancipation" that Jefferson hoped for? Did it clarify the purposes or elevate the ends of a free society? The answer as I see it is again yes and no, to an always uncertain extent. But again I think we need first to review the illiberal influences of organized religion, which were the most conspicuous in the last century, and which still color much contemporary thought. Here I take my text from Rabbi Abraham Heschel: "It is customary to blame secular science and antireligious philosophy for the eclipse of religion in modern society. It would be more honest to blame religion for its own defeats. Religion declined not because it was refuted, but because it became irrelevant, dull, oppressive, insipid."

At the outset of the century Chateaubriand had indicated a high hope in his most popular Genius of Christianity. Subtitled The Beauty of the Christian Religion, it dwelt not so much on the literal truth of Christianity as on its sentiment and poetry, symbolized by Gothic art. Conceived as poetry, it could become less dogmatic, more mellow; and Chateaubriand himself aspired to a "renovation" of Christianity, a reconciliation with ideals of liberty and progress. However, the Romantic revival did not inspire notable religious art in the nineteenth century. There was rather a marked deterioration in such art, especially in ecclesiastical taste. One reason was that the churches did not welcome efforts at renovation. They lagged behind intellectual as well as social and political developments; their major concerns came to seem increasingly irrelevant when not alien or oppressive. They bring us to another dreary story—the conflict between science and religion. By now most of us might agree that it was a quite unnecessary conflict, since science as science says nothing about the essential claims of the religious spirit, has no means whatever of either proving or disproving assertions about the ultimate; but the disagreeable truth remains that there was a bitter conflict, that it had abiding consequences, and indeed that it still raises troublesome questions.

Religious men had plenty of legitimate complaint about the kind of thought that claimed the authority of science: the many variants of a materialistic, mechanistic philosophy that depreciated all spiritual values, of a determinism that denied human freedom, of a positivism that branded all unverifiable statements as meaningless, and so on. They could dwell on the limitations of scientific knowledge, its obvious inadequacy for our living purposes; for science as such cannot teach us wisdom, tell us how best to use all the knowledge and power it gives us, nor can we strictly verify any of the values we live by. Unfortunately, churchmen chose to do battle primarily on behalf of dogmas that conflicted with new knowledge. They—not the scientists—were the aggressors; so they doomed themselves to a steady, humiliating retreat, losing battles out of which they salvaged only an embarrassing kind of popular success. Thus they fought the theory of evolution, which today is accepted by the great majority of educated Christians; their popular success is indicated by the fact that the major biological theory cannot be taught openly in most American high schools, or even mentioned in most school textbooks. (Cagey authors insinuate the idea by substituting for "evolution" the good sturdy American word "development"—perhaps suggesting that God is as respectable as other realtors.) Likewise churchmen fought the theories of Freud, primarily on behalf of the sexual taboos ingrained in Christian ethics. They manifestly did not succeed in preserving the sacred or impure mysteries of sex, but at least simple Christians still know that Freud taught wicked nonsense; while by now neo-orthodox thinkers have come around to welcoming his basic theory of the unconscious as a restatement of the doctrine of original sin, which to ordinary Americans has no vital meaning.[2]

More pertinent today is a broader, deeper conflict due to the spread of the scientific spirit. This led to extensive historical research into early Christianity, and in particular to the "higher criticism" of the Bible as a human, historical document. Many Christian scholars embarked on such studies, in which German Lutheranism was especially active. The outcome was the movement known as Modernism: a movement that embraced many varieties of belief and degrees of commitment, but that in general managed an accommodation with science by surrendering the traditional belief in the literal, infallible truth of the Bible, regarding it as divinely inspired only in a broad sense. Today, I assume, most thoughtful, educated Christians are Modernists of sorts, even if they do not call themselves by this name; the changes in attitude and belief have become so pervasive that they

[2] For Catholics an embarrassing instance was an article by Claire Booth Luce some years ago in a popular women's magazine, written after her religious conversion. She made out that the major villains in modern intellectual history were Marx, Freud, and Einstein. (The gentle Einstein got into her unholy trinity because she mistook his theory of relativity for a denial of absolute standards of truth.) She did not refrain from noting that her three villains were Jews.

are often unconscious, and these people do not realize that they would have been eligible for burning in the Middle Ages. Nevertheless, Modernism was continually fought by orthodox churchmen, and it still meets strong opposition. In this century it provoked the Protestant reaction of Fundamentalism, an uncompromising old-time religion that commands the authority of Karl Barth as well as much popular support. In the Catholic church, Modernism was officially stamped out by Pope Pius X (1903–14), who swore all priests to oppose such heresies as that Catholic dogmas "are not fallen from heaven" and that "Christian society is subject, like every human society, to a perpetual evolution." One sign of his apparent success is that Catholicism still numbers many fewer scientists of note, in proportion to its membership, than does Protestantism. The Church went on to proclaim the dogma that the Virgin went bodily to heaven—a dogma unsupported by a shred of either biblical or historical evidence, which might seem like a deliberate affront to modern thought.

Throughout this conflict, the fundamental issue for liberals and men of science was the intellectual freedom and intellectual integrity required by the pursuit of truth—a cause that seemed to them holy too. If churchmen were no longer able to censor the press, they could and did exert much public pressure, resort to more or less terrorist methods. (Thus in France Renan lost his university chair for publishing his unconventional *Life of Jesus*, while in England even John Stuart Mill did not dare to publish during his lifetime his unorthodox views on religion, for fear of jeopardizing the social and political causes that were his primary concern.) Churchmen aggravated the issue by branding honest disagreement or doubt as sinful, a moral offense—an attitude that persists in most ordinary Christians, for whom the word "freethinker" still connotes a disreputable type. More broadly, religion remained a primary source of the anti-intellectualism that has flourished ever since the Romantic movement, and that has scarcely promoted moral emancipation.

Otherwise, spokesmen of religion have persistently confused the issues of culture and spiritual values by claiming a monopoly on such values, as on moral truths. They have too often been blind to the religious quality of science, which many still describe as materialistic, while the rant of popular preachers passes for spirituality. For the scientific spirit is more disinterested than the conventional religious spirit, seeking truth for its own sake; it may also be humbler in its wonder, its respect both for fact and for mystery; and it can afford a kind of "spiritual freedom," beyond an emancipation from superstitious fear. Among the eloquent expressions of such freedom is that of the agnostic Thomas Huxley to his clerical friend Charles Kingsley. When Huxley's son died, Kingsley asked him if he did not now regret having given up the belief in personal immortality, a belief to which mankind had been led by its highest aspirations. "What is this," answered Huxley, "but in grand words asking me to believe a thing because I like it?" He went on: "Science seems to me to teach in the highest and strongest manner the great truth which is embodied in the Christian conception of entire surrender to the will of God. Sit down before fact as a little child, be prepared to give up every preconceived notion, follow humbly wherever and to whatever abysses Nature leads, or you shall learn nothing. I have only begun to learn content and peace of mind since I have resolved at all risks to do this."

Yet for most men, I should now add, the faith of Huxley clearly would not suffice; and their apparent need of more positive supernatural assurances brings up the difficult questions. Whitehead pointed to these when he lamented that churchmen

had not welcomed new knowledge and new theories in the spirit
of scientists. They should have seen in the clash of doctrines
an opportunity, not a disaster; for like science, religion has been
a continuous development, and its essence is the search for God,
a vision of some "final good" that is real yet "beyond all reach."
As a spirit of quest, I take it, the religious spirit may be respected
by all truth-seekers; and only by some such view of it can one
hope to do justice to the whole religious history of mankind,
and to the fundamentally different views of the great religious
teachers. Yet Whitehead's lofty ideal calls for serious qualifica-
tion. Many a holy man who may have begun as a seeker of God
or the ineffable truth ended as something rather different. Especially in Judaeo-Christian tradition, the great prophets and saints
spoke not as inquirers or seekers but as men of flaming conviction,
able to speak in the name of the one true God, to spell out quite
positively what he demanded of men; and while typically they
were themselves critical of the priesthood, they were not inclined
to permit any basic disagreement with their teachings, what they
saw as idolatry or the worship of false gods, or what we might
call freedom of worship. One can scarcely imagine Amos and
Jeremiah, Jesus and St. Paul, St. Bernard and St. Francis, welcoming a clash of doctrines. Much less have the established
churches been animated by a spirit of quest; their stock in trade
has typically been ritualism and legalism—the forms as typically
denounced by the great founders and prophets. And if thereby
they have always to some extent debased religion, they have in-
disputably served the needs of most men. The simple worshiper
is no quester. What he wants most of all—beyond an answer to
his prayers—is certainty, security, the ancient rock amid the shifting tides. He wants freedom from all doubt and anxiety.

In our day such wants are being emphasized more than they

ever were in the past. Churchmen themselves dwell not merely on the truth but the *need* of faith, or in effect the utility of religion. While many seem pleased to repeat that there were no atheists in the foxholes during the war (as if frightened men proved the reality of God), they betray the fact that faith is not actually so strong and vital as it once was; for a religious people never have to be told that they *need* to believe in God. We are brought to the most difficult question—the social consequences of the widespread decay of religious faith.

In the Victorian age the growth of doubt and disbelief was a burning issue, fought out in hundreds of popular novels as well as in the pulpits.[3] Science obviously had much to do with this skepticism, weakening faith not only by its heretical findings about man and the universe but by its essential spirit, its insistence on evidence and refusal to accept on authority; for the Bible remains the ultimate basis of Christianity's claim to truth. There is no question that many men suffered from their doubt or disbelief, since they still wanted to believe; students of the Victorians now emphasize the deep disquiet beneath their apparent complacency, lost on a "darkling plain swept with confused alarms of struggle and flight." It is important to realize that agnosticism means not merely suspended judgment but a kind of positive commitment, a surrender of whatever goods religious faith can offer—and without the compensation of atheism, an inverted religion that is commonly a fighting faith. Hence among the plainest consequences of the loss of faith was the common pessimism of modern literature, a deep sense of the ultimate meaninglessness of man's life in a universe wholly indifferent

[3] An excellent documentary study is Margaret M. Maison's *Victorian Vision: Studies in the Religious Novel* (New York: Sheed & Ward, 1962).

to his purposes, in which it has been said that life itself may be only "a disease that afflicts matter in its old age." Often the pessimism was made more corrosive by a denial of the dignity of man, due in part to further findings of science about glands, hormones, complexes, and other unprepossessing constituents of the human spirit. All this deepened anxiety, the marked tendencies to neurosis in the modern world; and a neurotic is not a free man.

Still, religions have also bred plenty of neurotics, Christianity perhaps more than any other by its historic emphasis on Satan and sin. Faith has always meant not only peace and joy but guilt, anxiety, fear; so to many young men especially, the loss of religious faith meant a feeling of emancipation, such as Somerset Maugham recorded in *Of Human Bondage*. They felt freer because Christian tradition had also aggravated the problem by its stress on the necessity for salvation of correct belief, and its endless, bitter controversy over what was correct belief. (Many pious Victorians were haunted chiefly by fears of Rome and the Jesuits.) Hence another plain consequence of the growing skepticism was the growth of intellectual freedom, more specifically freedom of speech and press, in the struggle for which enemies of the churches were most active. Christianity was itself awakened and to some extent revitalized by the necessity of defending itself. Most orthodox churchmen indeed continued to brand disbelief as irresponsible or immoral, and thereby to evade the real problem, the simple inability of many honest men to believe in God; their common policy of defending their faith by merely reasserting its absolute truth and absolute necessity tended to substantiate the schoolboy's definition of faith, as believing what you know ain't so. Many Christians, however, recognized the need for respecting the scientific spirit, and sought a more reasonable defense in the more liberal creed of Modernism. Because "liberal" is a good word in the context of this study, I should add that it may not be so to the deeply religious; for it may signify a cool, vague, or shallow faith, a loss of wholehearted commitment, and the tolerance it disposes men to has been nourished, no doubt, as much by religious indifference as positive conviction. Nevertheless, tolerance has become a matter of conviction for many Christians, and in any case it is better suited to a free society than the once general belief that a man's salvation depended upon his denomination. It has helped to offset the confusion and anxiety due to the loss of religious faith. Blind faith is of doubtful value to a free society, but bigotry is of no value whatever.

Meanwhile popular religion was showing up more serious shortcomings of the churches. To say that most men cannot be satisfied by the faith of Thomas Huxley is also to suggest that they have not been seriously infected by the scientific spirit, and that religion has suffered much more from a simple, popular kind of materialism. The decay of faith has been due most plainly to the rule of money values and the money spirit, the primacy of business in modern society, the basic inconsistency between the Christian gospel and the gospel of a profit system. Churchmen who attacked science were in general friendlier to this economic gospel. Organized religion accommodated itself much more readily to bourgeois values than it did to new knowledge; so it tended to become insipid, or in Whitehead's words, "to degenerate into a decent formula wherewith to embellish a comfortable life." Similarly it accommodated itself to the growth of nationalism, perhaps the most vital religion of the modern world. Until the rise of atheistic communism, the churches placed God squarely on both sides in every war.

They have therefore tended to obscure or confuse a more subtly troublesome problem of modern culture—the recognition of the relativity of values. This was no real problem until the nineteenth century, when history became a major branch of study and Hegel in particular made men aware of the fundamental importance of change. Accordingly, there arose the historical-mindedness that is now familiar, but that amounted to another revolution in thought—the awareness that art, literature, religion, and all institutions and beliefs are products of culture, and that none can be fully understood until it has been placed and dated, seen in relation to a historic process. The implications of relativity in this historicism were later accentuated by the new sciences of sociology and anthropology, whose practitioners generally insist that we have no right to judge the values of different cultures—we are all "culture-bound." I find that almost all my students, including the many who think of themselves as good Christians or Jews, disavow any absolute standards of truth, goodness, and beauty; though some begin to look dismayed when I ask them if, then, they believe that their religious faith is only a local custom. And all of us who are devoted to the free society might be troubled by further questions. Are ideals of freedom and justice merely local, cultural prejudices? Have we no right to speak of human rights—the rights of man as man? Dare we say flatly that Hitler's extermination of the Jews was "inhuman," absolutely evil, no less because it was an old Christian custom? Can we, with a clear intellectual conscience, object to the tyranny of communism, even though tyranny is much older and more nearly universal than democracy?

Yet I should stress first of all the value of an awareness of the actual relativity of values. Another word for relativism is pluralism, which means ideally a wider range of choice, more freedom of choice, richer potentialities for self-expression and self-realization. Immediately it makes for tolerance, breadth and openness of mind, sympathetic understanding of the many different ways of life—for attitudes that are now absolutely essential to hopes of world order and peace, in a world still ridden by national, cultural, and religious prejudice. As I read Western history I am impressed chiefly by the dangers of Christian absolutism, revealed in the long record of bigotry, fanaticism, and religious hatred, the most appalling record of persecution in religious history. At any rate, most churchmen failed to meet the challenge of relativity. They simply reaffirmed the absolute truths of Christianity, invoking the authority of the Bible: a sacred knowledge that has been revealed to a minority of mankind, and on the proper interpretation of which Christians themselves have never been able to agree. Still less have they ever agreed on the application of their absolute truths to social and political problems, just as only in the last hundred years have their church leaders come around to identifying Christian and democratic principles.

One may accordingly question the common charge of religious thinkers today that relativism has been undermining the spiritual basis of democracy. Relativists cannot indeed logically assert that democracy embodies absolute, universal rights of man; but there is no logical reason why they should not prefer it; there is much more apparent reason why they should oppose authoritarianism or totalitarianism—as generally in fact they have. Absolutists are logically more disposed to authoritarianism, and in fact have been throughout Western history. Today I know of no evidence that orthodox or fundamentalist Christians are the staunchest champions of democracy, but I have read considerable evidence that they are not very staunch defenders of civil liberties. And other fervent absolutists are Communists. Although Marx's dialectical materialism implies historical relativity, he himself concluded that his philosophy was objectively valid, positively true, and the Communists have erected it into a gospel; while they may disagree over their interpretations of their scripture, just as Christians always have, on principle they permit no more open dissent on fundamentals than Christians used to. In this respect, too, godless communism is a kind of religion: an old-fashioned kind, but on the face of it not antiquated.

Fortunately, the purposes of this study do not oblige me to resolve the problem of the relative and the absolute. My context, however, suggests a possible middle ground where it may look more difficult but also less disastrous. The Christian faith itself, to repeat, does not and cannot give positive answers to all practical questions. Thus the Ten Commandments (which incidentally have nothing to do with democracy) are largely accepted by all civilized societies, and in practice are necessarily qualified by all; the commandment not to kill is only the most obvious example —in wartime it is a patriotic duty to kill. As Byrum Carter sums it up, "The believer is committed; he is committed to seek to do good, and he knows that love is involved in doing good. He knows no more than this." On the other hand, the social scientist who denies the right to absolute judgments is no less committed to positive values, beginning with the values of the scientific spirit, and of intellectual honesty and freedom. Philosophical relativists and absolutists may at least agree that reliable knowledge and clear thinking are helpful in making the value judgments we all have to make anyway, and also that there is an important difference between fallible but honest thought and unreasoned prejudice. And so almost all thoughtful men may deplore a vulgar, sloppy kind of relativism that points to the most glaring defects of democratic culture.

The democratic sentiment that every man is entitled to his own opinion and taste has been muddied by the anarchic assumption that any opinion is as good as any other, and that it makes no difference what one likes so long as one is happy. In the present state of American culture the problem as I see it is not the acceptance of relative standards, but the common indifference to any standards of excellence. Certainly it is not an excess of tolerance or open-mindedness; ordinary Americans remain hostile enough to unbelievers and radicals, suspicious of "eggheads" and "pinkos," resentful of critics of the trash they feed their minds on. In a vague but important sense they remain absolutists, sure enough of the rightness of their own opinions, above all of the absolute superiority of the American way of life over all other ways. At the same time, their opinions and tastes are not really their own. Madison Avenue and the mass media inculcate the absolute values of conformity—of thinking, feeling, liking, wanting what everybody does; the most apparent exception is the appeal to snob values, which breeds only a more vulgar illusion of individuality, possibly a nastier kind of self-righteousness. In short, the serious complaint about the behavior of free Americans is that they are neither good relativists nor good absolutists, but so often appear unwilling or unable to make their own reasoned choices in values. The supreme goal is to be "well-adjusted," and it is best achieved by taking no thought about the kind of life, of people, or of God that one is becoming adjusted to.

In this view, lastly, I take up the now popular theme of moral corruption, with the popular thesis that the decay of morals is due to the decay of religious faith. It is a highly pertinent theme, since the maintenance of a free society requires a more responsible citizenry than the merely obedient subjects of monarchs or dictators. I should therefore note at once that it has been popular ever since the dawn of Western civilization. In every century writers and preachers have denounced the shocking sinfulness of their society; so one may gather that religion and morals have been decaying steadily for a thousand years. A historian may gather instead how hard it is to size up the actual state of either in any given society. Beneath the invariable divergent and conflicting trends, the basic religious and ethical beliefs may be fairly clear; but the questions always remain how vital the accepted creed was, how closely it corresponded with practical belief, how deeply it was felt, to what extent it governed behavior. The answer can never be certain, beyond the commonplace that no society has ever lived up to any of the higher religions. Otherwise the historic record chiefly belies popular assumptions. There is certainly no correlation between the state of morals and the flowering of culture, as the brilliant, scandalous Italian Renaissance makes sufficiently clear; but neither is there any clear, uniform correlation with the apparent state of religion.

Now, the overwhelming majority of men in the Western democracies still subscribe formally to Christian ethics, or more precisely to one of the varieties of such ethics. Religion plainly colors public opinion, which is always the most potent factor in determining motives and goals. No less plainly, however, popular faith is to a considerable extent merely formal. All but the most complacent would agree, I suppose, that religious faith is not so vital in modern America as it was in the Middle Ages, when Christendom devoted an infinitely larger proportion of its wealth and energy to glorifying its God. But this forces the immediate question: Are modern Americans more sinful or corrupt than medieval men were?

My guess is that on the whole they are more decent, better behaved. In some respects they are distinctly less gross and brutal than were medieval men; if they relish too much the second-hand violence in their comics and TV programs, they at least would not put up with such public spectacles as the torture and burning of heretics, or the autos-da-fé of Jews, by which churchmen once edified the faithful. Likewise the current crime waves hardly compare with the routine violence of the Middle Ages. In other respects Americans may appear less humble, patient, or stoical, but their want of the traditional virtues of poverty is offset by relative freedom from the meanness, coarseness, and bestiality that also spring from poverty and ignorance. Altogether, it is at least certainly not clear that Americans are either less law-abiding or less virtuous by Christian standards. Only the most sentimental medievalist can believe that men in the "Age of Faith" lived in a Christian spirit; for greed, lust, violence, and cruelty are written all over the medieval record, and the Church itself became scandalously corrupt, to an extent simply unthinkable in the modern secular world.[4]

More to the point, it does not seem clear to me either that Americans are more corrupt than they were a century ago, when presumably they were more religious or at least were more faithful churchgoers. Corruption in government and business has

[4] The record also suggests that Americans might not behave better if they really feared hell, as the Pope some years ago said all Christians needed to. Fear is not a moral motive anyhow, but the scandalous behavior of medieval men intimates that it promotes virtue no more than it does freedom. Rather, the literal belief in hell-fire helps to explain their common cruelty, including the atrocities sanctioned by the Church, since no treatment could be too harsh for sinners whom God himself sentenced to eternal torture. Otherwise, fear was offset by custom or public opinion that effectually minimized the danger of damnation for many common kinds of sin. Fornication, for example, seems to have been much more common in the Middle Ages than it is in sex-conscious America today, and for that matter it remains more common in such countries as Mexico, where about half the children are born illegitimate.

never been more flagrant than it was during and after the Civil War; today it may seem worse because Americans have set higher standards of responsibility in politics and big business. The behavior of ordinary men remains much harder to gauge, but I judge that at worst they have grown somewhat more complacent in their materialism, more self-indulgent, more inured to the routine hypocrisies of commercialism, to sloppy or dishonest workmanship, and the like. Other apparent changes, such as the revolt against Victorian respectability, the decline of the "Protestant ethic," and the growth of "togetherness," are morally ambivalent, not signs of mere degeneracy. In any case, the most apparent reason for any softening of moral fiber remains not the loss of religious belief but the reign of money values, the celebration of the profit motive, the irresponsibility of Madison Avenue and the mass media. The godless Russians have upheld a more puritanical morality (though with material success they too are beginning to look more bourgeois). The churches generally attacked only the symptoms, not the main sources, of materialism; and now the popular theme that only religious faith can preserve or restore morality might remind us that through the centuries preachers dwelt chiefly on the failure of Christians to behave properly. The most vigorous critics of modern society and culture have generally been secular writers.

These writers suggest another important reservation. Skepticism, relativism, and other such reputedly subversive tendencies have been most conspicuous among the well educated and thoughtful; and such people have generally been least prone to the popular corruptions of materialism. Few except Fundamentalists, I assume, would maintain that unbelievers are typically less upright than orthodox believers or churchgoers. Most people who have given up Christian dogma have held to Christian

43

ethics. If some became more open to sophisticated vices, others became more devoted to ethical ideals simply because these lacked supernatural sanctions, or were purged of such strictly un-ethical motives as the hope of eternal reward or fear of eternal damnation. Lord Acton offered another striking instance when George Eliot died. He then took a thousand more notes, cen-tered on the theme—to him still a little startling, even dismaying —that an unbeliever could be capable of such moral earnestness and loftiness as she exemplified; not to mention that she was much more liberal than his good friend Cardinal Newman.

Altogether, we unquestionably have to pay a considerable price for our secular culture in a free society. Art, literature, philosophy, and science remain autonomous; on principle we separate church and state, keep religion out of the public schools; and as we sur-vey the resultant disunity, disharmony, discord, we may recall the prophetic lament of John Donne over the rise of the "new philos-ophy" of natural science represented by Galileo: " 'Tis all in pieces, all coherence gone." In particular we have to pay the in-escapable costs of free thought and scientific inquiry, which among other things have led not only to much disagreeable knowledge but to a painful self-consciousness about the condi-tions of our thought. Even before World War I Croce wrote that we can no longer believe in a happy future for man on earth, or happiness in an afterlife, and that *"What we have alone retained is the consciousness of ourselves, and the need to make that con-sciousness ever clearer and more evident,* a need for whose satis-faction we turn to science and to art." There would appear to be no possibility whatever of re-establishing a Christian culture com-parable to medieval culture. Science alone makes it unthinkable, for scientific inquiry cannot operate on religious premises; the physicist does not seek guidance in Scripture or the will of God when he puzzles over the behavior of electrons, and no more can social scientists when they study social behavior. At most we might achieve what Paul Tillich call a "theonomous" culture—one not dominated by religious authority, but suffused by "an ultimate concern and a transcending meaning."

To this possibility I shall return in my concluding chapter. Meanwhile I should say that our cultural situation does not to me seem intolerable. Secular independence has made possible a singular breadth and variety of interest, a singularly bold and continuous creativity; it has been too often disparaged by churchmen who regard the secular as irreligious instead of merely non-religious; and its costs have been magnified by the sentimental piety of traditionalists, especially the fashion of glorifying the Middle Ages that has come down from the Romantic movement. There was, after all, plenty of disunity, disharmony, discord in the "Age of Faith."

❖ III ❖

RELIGIOUS REVOLUTIONARIES
KIERKEGAARD AND DOSTOEVSKI

SINCE I HAVE BEEN dwelling chiefly on the conservative tendencies of established Christianity, it is time to recall that the gospel preached by Jesus was strictly radical, and that if taken literally it is still revolutionary. Like the great prophets of Israel, he attacked the ruling class, the high priests, the respectable men of his day; it was not "the mob" alone that crucified him. When Christianity eventually became the imperial religion of the Greco-Roman world, its Church in turn had trouble with many ardent spirits, who were repelled by its worldly compromises. With the rise of Western civilization the gospel began breeding a long line of heretics and rebels, who might be saintly, might be fierce or fanatical, but always were subversive types, and more often than not appealed mainly to the poor, as Jesus had. Within the Church, too, there were always some who maintained the prophetic tradition of self-criticism. Among its major consequences was Protestantism, which at once began breeding more troublemakers within its own ranks; Martin Luther was infuriated by the heretical Anabaptists. Hence one might expect some radical responses of Christianity to the revolutionary modern world, the more so because its established churches were naturally conservative. It in fact helped to inspire many agitators and utopian dreamers. But it also produced some revolutionary thinkers of a different sort, most notably Kierkegaard and Dostoevski: "modern" men who were quite unlike Jesus in spirit, but who alike rebelled against modern civilization in his name. They launched a criticism of it that was in some respects more fundamental than the criticism of Karl Marx, and that still applies to both democratic and communistic societies.

Now about Kierkegaard (1813–55) I should at once confess that while I can appreciate why he has deeply impressed men I respect, I am not myself so impressed. I am often bored by his repetitiousness, sometimes repelled by his apparent obsessions, and I am not always sure that I understand the "dialectical theology" on which he prided himself. I must leave to the reader, for example, the "transparency" of his key definition of faith: "By relating itself to its own self and by willing to be itself, the self is grounded transparently in the Power which constituted it."[1] Yet there is little question about the basic ideas that have made him a major influence on modern religious thought, as well as on existentialism, the popular philosophy of our day. There seems to me little question either of the major bearings of his thought on issues of freedom, my primary concern here. That he had but a slight influence in his day, coming into his own only in our century, testifies to his originality; but we can now place him in broad currents of thought that flowed from the Romantic movement, and that all through the nineteenth century were swirling with problems we have lately become more keenly aware of.

---

[1] In fairness to myself, I might add that his translators have disagreed over the precise meaning of the phrase here rendered as "relating itself to its own self" (translation by Walter Lowrie). They also acknowledge that he can be difficult or "elusive."

47

Among the most important of these currents was the revulsion against the rationalism of the Age of Enlightenment. The Romantics first restored the claims of sentiment, intuition, and imagination, in the interests of the elemental, non-rational needs of man, including his religious needs; but their attack broadened into a profound critique of reason that remained a major theme of nineteenth-century thought. With the rise of psychology and the social sciences in our century we have acquired a much clearer consciousness of the actual limitations of the power of reason, for both theoretical and social purposes—limitations that supporters of a free society can never afford to minimize. To this movement Kierkegaard contributed something as a kind of depth psychologist, who in flashes anticipated Freud. Mainly, however, his attack on intellect sprang from his devotion to faith, "the highest passion in a man." He condemned the abstractness of the God of the philosophers, exemplified by the World Spirit of Hegel (who long before Nietzsche remarked that God was dead). He insisted that faith could never be comprehended by reason, and that it transcended rational ethics as well as practical wisdom. Its perfect symbol was Abraham, who at the Lord's bidding prepared to sacrifice his beloved son Isaac—to commit what by ordinary ethical standards was murder. Kierkegaard asserted that faith begins in "the absurd," a basic absurdity that he erected into a cardinal principle, and that existentialists would make much of. In other words, he stressed the basic paradoxes of the Christian faith. So Abraham was "greater than all, great by reason of his power whose strength is impotence, great by reason of his wisdom whose secret is foolishness, great by reason of his hope whose form is madness, great by reason of the love which is hatred of oneself." In Scripture such faith was summed up in the hard saying attributed to Jesus by Luke: "If any man cometh unto me and hateth not his own father and mother and wife and children and brethren and sisters, yea, and his own life also, he cannot be my disciple."

This uncompromising spirit intensified Kierkegaard's criticism of organized religion, which he attacked as bitterly as did the godless Nietzsche after him. The Christian churches were naturally worldly, respectable institutions, but he despised them the more because they were preaching an easy, comfortable kind of faith suited to an increasingly bourgeois society. They were reducing the service of God to a conventional morality, including such vulgar teachings as that virtue paid; they were praising men for going to church now and then, as if this were doing God a great honor; they were in his view ever heightening the injustice that had been done to Jesus Christ by naming Christendom after him. Whereas Martin Luther had ninety-five theses, he wrote, "I should have only one, that Christianity does not exist." He added that the lives of most men were "too spiritless even to be called in a strictly Christian sense sin."

A further reason why Kierkegaard could never abide organized religion was his primary concern for the individual or the self, the root of his existentialist philosophy. This came out of Protestant tradition, of course, but its immediate source was the Romantic movement, in the preoccupation of both poets and philosophers with the subjective. "Truth is subjectivity," Kirkegaard said flatly. He identified it with "the passion of the infinite" (another characteristically Romantic passion), which he described as "the decisive factor." He added, "Only in subjectivity is there decisiveness, to seek objectivity is to be in error." In simpler, possibly less dubious terms, he asserted that the only reality that concerned a man was his own conscious existence. For the Christian this meant that one should maintain an absolute relation to God as an individual, not through such intermediaries as state and church or such abstractions as humanity or mankind. "The Christian heroism," Kierkegaard concluded, "is to venture wholly to be oneself, as an individual man, this definite individual man, alone before the face of God, alone in this tremendous exertion and this tremendous responsibility."

Such exertion and responsibility implied the most popular of his ideas today, the concept of *Angst* or dread. A man can become really conscious of his own being only through "fear and trembling"; he must learn that "to exist as the individual is the most terrible thing of all." Kierkegaard accordingly insisted that despair was the natural condition of all men outside Christendom, and of most men within it. Almost all lived in despair, no less if they thought they were secure and contented; for one form of despair was precisely not being aware of it. It marked the great majority of men who never became fully conscious that they were spiritual beings, real individuals, and so led wasted, defrauded lives. By the same token, however, despair was not for Kierkegaard the upshot. All men had to struggle with *Angst* if they were to become aware of their being, but they could and should master it, win their way to Christian faith. To live either in dread or in unawareness of one's being was an offense against God, the author of our being. Kierkegaard defined sin as "to be in despair at not willing to be oneself, or in despair at willing to be oneself."

Sinners should also realize that this sketchy account does nothing like justice to the richness of his thought. It may suggest most clearly the reasons why Kierkegaard is so often prolix, difficult, and elusive; for while he insisted that faith could never be comprehended by reason, he nevertheless sought to make it comprehensible in a dozen books, all very heady, in which he also sought to demonstrate the objective validity of a truth he declared was subjective. But at least he was no mystic, trying to utter an ineffable or unutterable truth; he kept appealing to concrete experience of a kind presumably available to all men, kept asserting the claims of an individual or a self presumably as real to all of us; and even a sketchy outline of his thought may suffice to indicate that its implications for a free society were ambiguous through and through.

His radical censure of Christendom, to begin with, has become a commonplace. If his uncompromising spirit made him unfair to the churches, they were manifestly accommodating themselves too readily to the materialism of the rising middle class, serving the interests of mere respectability, supporting a peculiarly mean kind of hypocrisy. No other great religion had ever lent such sanctity to the acquisition of property as Christianity now did. The popular tendency to equate religion with morality was more insidious in a complacent class that emphasized what worked or what paid, and was on its way to the popular belief that to be a good Christian one had only to be a good fellow, a good Elk. Kierkegaard recalls the service that religion may do a free society as a critic of its means and ends, and today as a critic of an affluence commonly lacking any lofty ends to speak of.

More obviously pertinent is his insistence on both the freedom and the responsibility of the individual. While laying down the law for man, he himself refused unconditional submission to any human authority, and the law declared that every man had a free choice and must make his own vital decisions. It affirmed an individualism more radical than had either Christian or secular liberal tradition. The paradoxes of faith included the idea that "the individual is higher than the universal," as Abraham demonstrated when he prepared to transgress the ethical law against murder. If this idea is clearly liable to abuse, as clearly it magnified the dignity of the individual, the grounds for his resistance to the tyranny either of government or of convention. At the same time, it magnified his responsibility both to God and to himself. It led Kierkegaard to another questionable doctrine, that "the crowd is untruth"; his scorn of the crowd usually implied contempt for "the masses" (even though in a footnote he stated that he meant only number or society at large), and it could embrace lofty appeals to the interests of "humanity." But immediately he was attacking chiefly the forces of convention and conformism, the tyranny of public opinion, the cowardice of seeking refuge in multitude. In pointing out that Scripture required man to love his neighbor, not the crowd, he remarked that love of one's neighbor called for self-denial, whereas loving or pretending to love the crowd was only a form of self-interest. Short of the God of Abraham, his gospel is much like Ralph Waldo Emerson's gospel of self-reliance, and may therefore be as bracing for unbelievers.

Today both believers and unbelievers might welcome in particular Kierkegaard's declared purpose to "create difficulties everywhere." He condemned all forms of complacent faith—in God or in man, in reason or in science—that enabled men to shirk their personal responsibilities, enjoy a shallow contentment or a false sense of security. It was never easy to be a good Christian; it took uncommon courage and honesty to have genuine faith; and no more was it easy to become a real individual, assume the responsibilities of freedom and selfhood. In an industrial mass society it has become harder to maintain personal integrity and personal independence, a mind and a life of one's own, and still less can free men afford any easy faith at a time of world crisis, with reasons for dread such as Kierkegaard hardly anticipated. Beset by appalling difficulties and dangers, most men—especially in the United States and in Russia—nevertheless appear to lack a sufficient sense of difficulty. In his own day Kierkegaard neither had nor wanted disciples, at least in the sense of followers devoted to any system or program for salvation; and one can scarcely imagine his ever having a large popular following. But we can understand why the works of "That Individual"—as he said he would like to be called in his epitaph, if any—have become something like a modern Bible, and why the many thinkers he has influenced include both religious and political liberals, such as Reinhold Niebuhr and Paul Tillich.

Still, he would unquestionably have condemned such liberals (not to mention such atheists as Sartre, among the oddly assorted thinkers known as existentialists). Kierkegaard was nothing of a liberal himself, in either theology or politics. For all his apparent subtlety and complexity, he was at bottom a rigid authoritarian, ultraconservative, in the long anti-intellectual tradition of Christianity that had come down through Martin Luther. The incomprehensible faith that he insisted on was not arrived at by intuition either, but rested simply on revelation. Although he granted that the truth of Christianity had been revealed "in an equally incomprehensible way," he permitted no serious question of it, no freedom to doubt. In *The Confusion of the Present Age* he asserted that "disobedience, unwillingness to obey" was the misfortune of his age. "One deceives oneself and others by wishing to make us imagine that it is doubt," he added. "No, it is insubordination."

As an archindividualist preaching a solitary way to salvation, Kierkegaard naturally rejected any thought of social or political solutions to the spiritual problems that concerned him, but as an authoritarian he specifically attacked the liberal, democratic tendencies of his day, branding them as another sign of grievous insubordination. His dread of them was confirmed by the popular revolutions of 1848, which in Denmark forced the monarch to grant constitutional government. Now the common people were subjecting both king and God to their will; so "the crowd" became "the mob." If he was repelled chiefly by the vulgarization of religion, he in any case displayed little of the spirit of Jesus, little compassion for the poor and lowly, and for social purposes made nothing of the gospel of the brotherhood of man.[2] Kierkegaard's aristocratic attitude was not due, either, to a concern for standards of culture, or what he rather loosely called "aesthetics." While he had a natural fondness for poetry and music, he came to fear all humanistic cultural interests as a distraction from revealed truth and the necessities of faith, or of despair. One must choose, he wrote in his *Journals*, "either to make aesthetics everything and so explain everything in that way, or religion." If a faith that passed understanding might not appear to explain much, it was all the more necessary because so many men in his age seemed content with "aesthetics."

Now, I doubt that Kierkegaard is to any significant extent

[2] It is not without significance (as a cautious scholar might say) that Walter Lowrie, the chief American translator of Kierkegaard and one of his most reverent admirers, also expressed a warm admiration of Mussolini. As late as 1940, in a book on St. Peter and St. Paul, Dr. Lowrie reminded Americans that God had sent his chosen people "a Duce like Moses," and that early Christians had "no prejudice at all" in favor of democracy; he lauded Mussolini for having achieved the spiritual regeneration of Italy, rescued it from Jewish Freemasonry, etc. I judge that Kierkegaard himself would have been disgusted by the vulgarity of Mussolini, but at least his disciples might logically prefer fascism to democracy since it exalted obedience and had no truck with insubordination.

directly responsible for the reactionary, authoritarian tendencies in modern thought. My impression is that his influence in this respect chiefly confirmed thinkers already headed that way; and the most dogmatic, such as ordinary Fundamentalists, would be as unlikely to read him as would dictators. Nevertheless, he has been widely and eagerly studied; he retains great prestige. Whatever his positive influence, he is especially suggestive for my purposes here; for his insistent paradoxes force the deepest and most difficult issues of religion in the modern world, the ambiguities underlying the relatively simple issues raised by organized and popular religion.

So let us reconsider Abraham, the perfect symbol of Kierkegaard's faith. The unquestioning faith of Abraham, prepared to sacrifice his dearest to his Lord, may indeed look sublime—until one considers Isaac, and considers him as no stooge but the innocent victim of this faith. Abraham is preparing not only to commit what men call murder, but to violate the Christian precept of the sanctity of the person. An admirer of Kierkegaard who notes that many biblical scholars regard this story as an early protest against human sacrifice answers that of course the master was not "bound to pedantic expositions of the obvious"; though like Kierkegaard he disregards another biblical story in which Abraham reasoned with God, pleaded with him not to destroy Sodom if there were just men in the city. But Kierkegaard was bound to answer the basic question raised by this willingness to do apparent evil in the name of the Lord. In his own words, "How then does the individual assure himself that he is justified?" And he gave no rational answer—he merely rejected rational criteria, calling in his principle of "the absurd." This is plainly a very dangerous principle in view of all the patent absurdities and barbarities that have been committed in the name of religion: the wholesale slaughters authorized by God in the Old Testament, the murders and atrocities blessed by the medieval Church and the Protestant reformers, the whole appalling record of Christian persecution. History suggests that another name for the unquestioning faith exalted by Kierkegaard may be blind faith, and that it can too readily deserve the worse name of fanaticism.

Such faith is still common enough to justify more pedantic expositions of the obvious, beginning with a simple refusal to believe that God ever commands men to violate their conscience. This of course involves a judgment of God by human standards, or what Kierkegaard denounced as an insult to God; but his resentment of all efforts to uphold the reasonableness of Christianity recalls the obvious dangers of the whole reaction against the rationalism of the Enlightenment in which he figured. He did not merely emphasize the limitations of reason—he was positively hostile to its claims, and therefore as hostile to science. He heralded the outright revolt against reason, which in our century has led to the glorification of the unconscious, the instinctive, the voice of the blood—the positively irrational. This seems to me a doubtful boon to the cause of Christianity; for the paradoxical power, wisdom, and hope that Kierkegaard celebrated in Abraham are in ordinary men likely to come out chiefly as impotence, foolishness, madness, and hatred. But certainly the revolt against reason has been no boon to the cause of a free society. Among its prophets was Adolf Hitler.

As dubious, accordingly, is a related dictum of Kierkegaard. "The conclusions of passion," he asserted, "are the only reliable ones, that is, the only convincing ones"; so he concluded, "What our age lacks is not reflection but passion." We might all agree that if reflection leads men to belief, passion is much closer to the heart of religious faith, and that no faith can be vital without it. We might also respect Kierkegaard's own "passion for the infinite" as a total commitment, the essence of faith, and his scorn of the spiritlessness of his bourgeois society, the devotion to ease, comfort, and "happiness" that many liberals complain of still more in our own society. Yet there always remain the obvious questions: Which passions? In the service of what faith? If the conclusions of passion are generally more convincing, on the record they are surely not at all reliable. Nor does a contemporary disciple clarify the issue when he adds that the "real danger" in modern times comes from ruthless, calculating rationalists. We all know of such types, but we should know too that their ambitions are ordinarily backed by sufficient passion, and that as leaders they do not appeal to reflection. We have only to ask: Was Hitler such a cold rationalist? If so, were his followers lacking in passion? On the face of it, we have scarcely suffered from a dearth of passion in this century, and there is still more than enough to go around.

Among its sources today is Kierkegaard's most popular concept of *Angst*. Here one might first remark that his insistence on the universality of despair was too easy, since he demonstrated it by arguing that despair is usually hidden, that a common form of it is "precisely" a sense of security and tranquillity, and that even a rich, intense aesthetic enjoyment of life is "after all despair"; by this method one can prove almost anything one has a mind to about the "real" feelings of men. More plainly, Kierkegaard's insistence suggests a morbid quality in his own faith, due immediately to his unhappy love affair and possibly involving some self-deception. (Among his unconscious paradoxes, incidentally, was his embarrassing sensitivity to public opinion, which he always professed to despise.) Thus he made dread a necessary condition of faith or true spirituality, while he dismissed apparent health of mind or spirit, and the whole tradition of Greek humanism, as either illusion or shallowness. He carried to the extreme the Christian tradition that emphasized suffering, guilt, and fear—all perhaps good for the soul of man, as for the prosperity of priesthoods, but not conducive to freedom of mind and spirit. Today there is more need of stressing such reservations simply because there are much more apparent reasons for anxiety or dread. In ordinary men *Angst* is likely to breed ugly passions, above all hate. Among intellectuals it has become so fashionable that it suggests a cult. In literary circles I have heard writers and thinkers dismissed with a single sentence—"He doesn't suffer from anxiety"; and while it appears that anxiety is the badge of intellectual responsibility or integrity, I get the impression that the badge is being worn with some unseemly self-pity. I think a free society might do better with less of such fear and trembling today and with a more resolute effort at freedom from *Angst*.

Kierkegaard himself, to be sure, insisted on the necessity of overcoming it, but thereby he brought up another difficulty more serious than he realized. The conditions he set remain strictly impossible for the great majority of mankind. Only some Christians may shudder their way to his God—an arbitrary God, known only by a revelation not granted to most men. The rest might concur in a final objection to his thought. "Eternity," he wrote characteristically, "asks of thee and of every individual among these million millions only one question, whether thou hast lived in despair or not, whether thou wast in despair in such a way that thou didst not know thou wast in despair. . . ." So he repeatedly reduced eternal difficulties to "only one question." As typically he phrased it in terms of either-or: either Abraham was absolutely right or he was lost, either you have God or you have no self, and so on. The final objection to Kierkegaard is that despite all his apparent complexity and "difficulty" he was at bottom much too simple. He evaded the really serious religious difficulties, beginning with the obvious reasons for honest doubt and radical disagreement. In particular he exemplified the simple arrogance that had always made Christianity liable to inhumanity. On sin and salvation he insisted on "the hollowness of every other definition which is not in the strictest sense Christian"—that is, in his own sense; so he automatically condemned to sin the whole pre-Christian world, and now the whole non-Christian world. He simply ignored the claims of all other religions.

For social purposes, there remains the obvious objection that Kierkegaard offered no basis for a new society, as he offered none for either rational inquiry or concerted effort to promote the common good. If all might profit from his criticism of the mediocrity of modern society, he went on to propose at most a way of life for some individuals that in effect relieved them of their obligations to their fellow men. One need not subscribe to the popular idea that criticism should always be constructive, not merely destructive, to ask more than this of a religious thinker in a revolutionary world. We are accordingly led to Dostoevski, another voice crying in the wilderness, but crying a way to social as well as personal salvation. Although he did not know the work of Kierkegaard, he had learned by himself all about *Angst*, the absurd, the paradoxes of faith, while as a revolutionary artist he created a world at once much grander and more awful than the self-centered Dane knew. Nevertheless, he returned to the simple Christian gospel of brotherhood and love. His message was radical because he took quite literally the teaching of Jesus, and insisted that nothing else could possibly do.

It should therefore be noted at once that Dostoevski's expressed faith was much simpler than Kierkegaard's in another, less edifying respect: whereas the latter remained forever critical of all organized religion, Dostoevski identified Christianity with the Russian Orthodox church, which he said alone preserved "the Divine image of Christ." This naïve faith involved not only fears, as naïve, that the Roman church would conspire with socialism against the Russian church but also some uglier simplicities. Dostoevski was a fervent jingo, who identified the church with the cause of Russia; he kept calling for holy wars on the Turks. Faithful to venerable tradition, he was also an anti-Semite. For the same reason he was no apostle of a free society but politically a simple reactionary: the Orthodox church had always supported absolute monarchy, sanctified the czar.

Such simplicities, however, were the message of Dostoevski as journalist and propagandist. None of his readers need to be told that as a novelist he was infinitely more sensitive, complex, and profound. He constantly dramatized ambiguity and difficulty, including all the difficulties evaded by Kierkegaard. He was a relentless analyst of men possessed by ideologies, the characteristic disease of modern thought; yet he knew that thoughtful men could hardly avoid ideology. He knew through his own torments the reasons for disbelief; in a letter he acknowledged that he was himself "a child of the age, a child of unfaith and doubt." The search for God that constituted a major theme of his last novels was no less an ordeal to the characters who represent his professed faith. When pressed hard by an atheist, Shatov in The Possessed stammers, "I . . . I will believe in God"—suggesting a desperate will to believe that falls short of Kierkegaard's "true" faith, but is truer to the experience of many honest, thoughtful men in the modern world. Above all, Dostoevski faced up to the mystery of pain and suffering, the everlasting problem of evil in a universe created by an all-powerful, all-knowing, all-good God. For Kierkegaard the mystery was no serious problem: chiefly it illustrated the "infinite, yawning, qualitative difference" between God and man that he insisted on, and the acceptance of absurdity that was the hallmark of faith. Dostoevski was much more troubled because he remained closer, if not truer, to a God of love who had appeared on earth in human form, and also because he took human history more seriously. Through Ivan Karamazov he presented one of the most eloquent statements of the problem of evil since the Book of Job; and many readers feel (as he himself feared) that he failed to answer as convincingly Ivan's negation of God's handiwork. He had a more tragic sense of life than any great Christian writer since Pascal.

This tragic sense deepened Dostoevski's otherwise familiar criticism of modern civilization—the materialism and hypocrisy of the West, its secularism, its faith in reason and science, etc. He exposed both the shallowness and the potential inhumanity of all the fashionable creeds that trusted to simple system or formal program, while slighting the simple necessities of a spirit of love and brotherhood. He knew beforehand the reasons why so many intellectuals would become disillusioned with their ideologies or -isms, especially Marxist socialism or communism. Liberals might have learned from him what many have lately discovered to their dismay, that the working class is not disposed to be liberal on matters not affecting their own material interests; to him one of the most deplorable products of a bourgeois society was a proletariat that aspired mainly to the status of good bourgeois. Similarly, Dostoevski was an acute critic of the Socratic tradition of rationalism that attributed evil and folly primarily to ignorance, and in particular a critic of the more widely popular gospel of individualism. His *Notes from Underground* was a prelude to existentialism as a remarkably original, revolutionary study of a very self-conscious man who prized above all his individuality, who was wretched in it, who quite knowingly and deliberately did evil, and who thereby only accentuated the purposelessness of his life, as of the society against which he rebelled.

At the same time, the "Underground Man" suggests a further critique of Kierkegaard. The latter's man of true faith was a self-centered man, aloof from "the crowd"; one apparent reason for his *Angst* was that he had little feeling of social solidarity, which in Dostoevski's view was essential to true security. Since the Underground Man, moreover, was as superior to merely rational ethics, as ready if need be to break the biblical commandment "Thou shalt not kill," how was he to tell possibly demonic impulse from divine inspiration? Dostoevski's indictment of the "terrible individualism" of the modern world sprang in part from a vivid sense of the demonic impulse in man, which again he knew in himself. And the impious Underground Man accentuated a still more basic difficulty for the religious. Kierkegaard's glorification of the individual, or the self that was the immediate source of passion and truth, did not clearly require a belief in his God, still less in a Bible whose authors rarely sounded like good existentialists; his philosophy might as logically lead to the atheism of Nietzsche and Sartre. Nietzsche in particular was another archindividualist who had much the same passion for greatness through self-reliance, the same scorn for convention and the common herd, and who incidentally was much impressed by *Notes from Underground;* but for such reasons he was an archenemy of Christianity, which had discouraged self-reliance by teaching men that they were lost without a Savior, cursing them with a sense of guilt and sin, filling them with *Angst,* while also flattering the cowardly herd with promises of eternal bliss in a life to come.

Nietzsche might therefore have been still more impressed by Dostoevski's celebrated parable of the Grand Inquisitor. Ostensibly this was an attack on the Roman Catholic church: in recognizing the Christ returned to earth but nevertheless sentencing him to death, the Grand Inquisitor argued that Christ had offered men a freedom that was an intolerable burden for the vast majority, who craved first of all bread, then "miracle, mystery, and authority"—the stock in trade of the Roman church. But the parable goes much deeper than mere polemic. The Grand Inquisitor here is not simply an evil old man, nor is he by any means speaking simply wicked nonsense. He is ominously prophetic, if perhaps more so than Dostoevski realized or intended; for he predicted that as a result of their unbearable freedom and their science, men would bring on a terrible confusion, destruction, "cannibalism"—the kind of hell we have gone through in the last generation. At least the parable forces a fundamental question. I have made it a main theme in my *History of Freedom* because throughout the history of civilization, as I read it, the great majority of men in fact lived by "miracle, mystery, and authority," often without enough bread, neither enjoying nor demanding the freedom we know. Today sociologists and psychologists tell us that what men primarily want is security, not freedom; we hear a good deal about the "escape from freedom," as about the craving for "togetherness"; and the future of the free society is uncertain if only because the question forced by the Grand Inquisitor remains wide open.

Yet the parable also points to the severe limitations of Dostoevski as a guide for a free society. He was hardly realistic in his devotion to the Russian Orthodox church, which was no less dedicated to miracle, mystery, and authority than was the Roman church.[3] He was more hopelessly unrealistic in his devotion to Holy Russia and its despotic czars, which came down to simple sentimentality over a mythical past. In this spirit he showed much less effective concern for the poor and lowly whom he enshrined in Christian brotherhood than did the liberals and the Socialists he attacked. He was content to chant his faith in the Russian peasant: again a sentimental faith in an idealized peasant, whose long endurance of grinding oppression he explained as greatness of soul, proved by "craving for suffering, perpetual and unquenchable suffering." While by such standards he damned Western civilization as shallow and corrupt, at home he supported some of its most dangerous tendencies, such as the growing nationalism, racism, and militarism that both Hitler and Stalin would exploit. And if the vulgar, brutal streak in Dostoevski was most apparent in his popular journalism, it nevertheless testified to a strained quality in his religious faith, which had not clearly brought him peace of mind or wisdom, spiritual freedom

[3] As an offshoot of the Holy Orthodox church, it brings up the reason why I am disregarding Eastern Christendom in this study. There is little to say here of the Holy Orthodox church other than that with the aid of the Ottoman Turks, who granted it full jurisdiction over their Orthodox subjects, it maintained the ultraconservative tradition it inherited from the Byzantine Empire. In gratitude to the Turks its leaders did not support the Greek war of independence early in the nineteenth century—an uprising that stirred much enthusiasm among partisans of freedom in Europe. Otherwise eastern Europe, excepting Russia, played an insignificant part in Western history until recent times.

or health. Even as a novelist he bedeviled the issues of the good life with some violent simplifications. He illustrated the alleged natural profundity of the brooding, suffering, soulful Russians by Ivan Karamazov's desperation over the conventional idea that morality depends on religion: if there is no God and immortal life, said Ivan, "everything is lawful." In historic fact, all societies have always had moral codes, with or without supernatural sanctions or promises of immortal life, and ethics is also logically prior to the higher religions, since one has to have some concept of good before he can say that God is good.

Hence both Kierkegaard and Dostoevski may suffer by comparison with the godless Nietzsche, another spiritual father of existentialism, who from the opposite pole condemned as roundly the bourgeois West. He had much more historical sense than either of them, and a deeper insight as a social critic; among other things, he scorned the vulgar idolatry of nation, state, and race to which Dostoevski succumbed. He may seem saner and more wholesome, too, despite his extravagances and his own dangerous gospel of the "superman." At least he valued sanity above a capacity for despair or a craving for suffering, and he rang out his lusty Yea to man's life in the face of as unflinching a tragic vision of life. He may therefore serve as an antidote to the possibly morbid cult of *Angst*, in which Kierkegaard and Dostoevski have come to rank as major prophets. I doubt that human freedom is quite so dreadful as Sartre and other existentialists make out by their metaphysical insistence on the separate, solitary self, and on the hostility of a universe that merely fails to guarantee man's values, leaves him alone to determine his own values. I sense both some self-deception and self-indulgence in the literary fashion of anxiety. Kierkegaard and Dostoevski did not subscribe to any such ostentation of *Angst* or surrender to it; but Nietzsche had a more robust spirit, and more roundly affirmed the values of self-respect and self-trust.

All of them, however, scorned the habit of compromise in the Western democracies. They may accordingly serve the interests of a free society by reminding us of the possible flabbiness of the liberal spirit, the usual muddle of middle ways, the frequent meanness of happy mediums, and all the mediocrity that makes it harder to live and let live. But they may also obscure the positive values of the liberal spirit, and the positive necessity of habits of compromise for the maintenance of a free society. The land of Dostoevski is the clearest case in point. For him Christ was the total solution; political reform was irrelevant, reason would never do, only love would do; and the ruthlessness of the atheistic Communists might seem to prove that without God everything indeed becomes lawful or permissible—just as both Ivan and the Underground Man concluded. The fact remains that no major society today is less permissive than the Soviet, more insistent on disciplined, strictly lawful behavior by its citizenry. Christians in the free world, who by and large seem slacker, might breathe more easily if Ivan were right. The Soviet illustrates rather the possible inhumanity of Dostoevski's scorn of the liberal creed, scorn of the kind of humility implicit in efforts at mere reasonableness. Or let us say that it confirms what he knew as a novelist, "a child of unfaith and doubt," that man is a "monstrous mixture" of good and evil, a creature of wondrous, fearful duality. For such a creature there can be no total, final solution; and the case for the free society may be based precisely on the mixed stuff in him. In the well-known words of Reinhold Niebuhr, "Man's capacity for justice makes democracy possible; but man's inclination to injustice makes democracy necessary."

⋅➤ IV ⤚⋅

RELIGION IN AMERICA

ALTHOUGH WE HAVE all heard too much about the uniqueness of American democracy, I still think we need to emphasize its native sources. Its basic principles of course came straight out of Western cultural tradition, including the Christian faith, and it has always been much more indebted to Europe than most Americans cared to realize; yet the point remains that America took to democracy long before Europe did. It was the first great nation consciously to be founded on the theories propagated by the Age of Enlightenment (a fact overlooked by many practical Americans who distrust "mere theory"). It was the first to translate the theoretical principle of equality into the political practice of universal suffrage. It was the first specifically to deny the state any right to interfere with religion or to favor any one church. And the most apparent reason why it took such novel steps was the conditions of life in a literally New World. Democratic ideals were backed by much stronger sentiments of equality and liberty in a land where there was no entrenched hereditary aristocracy, common men enjoyed much more opportunity than they did in the Old World, and the moving frontiers fostered more actual equality and liberty.

At the same time, such uniqueness is not simply a matter for pride. It also implies that American democracy was not founded on pure idealism, Christian or otherwise, and it indicates why America became a world symbol of materialism, why it has long rejoiced in the fond belief that it could worship both God and Mammon. Thus its gospel of individualism, which is perhaps the clearest example of how Protestantism has helped to promote personal freedom, flourished on the realities of pioneering life, then on the opportunities for developing or exploiting the immense resources of a continent; but for the same reason it was more easily corrupted by a gospel of self-seeking, since the plainest opportunities were economic, the plainest end in view was the almighty dollar. Likewise the idea of progress was no mere philosophical theory of history in America but an excited feeling, a living faith sprung from the conspicuous progress in a land of wide open spaces; and thereby it became a naïve, uncritical faith in a primarily material progress.

And so with the growth of religious freedom in America, the emergence of the first great pluralistic society in the Western world. Everybody except one hundred per cent patriots knows that the Puritans came to Massachusetts seeking freedom only for themselves, and soon proved that they were as intolerant as any Christians had ever been. With few exceptions, American colonists everywhere had little if any respect for fundamental differences in religious opinion, had no idea that all men should enjoy complete religious freedom. Ever since, there has always been enough prejudice and ill feeling to fill volumes, such as Gustave Myer's *History of Bigotry in the United States*. The most apparent reason why Americans incorporated the principle of religious freedom in their Constitution was again the compelling facts of their national life. Within a century the colonists numbered many different sects. Among them were some men, like Roger Williams and the Quaker William Penn, who believed in toleration on principle, but the rest simply had to tolerate religious differences if they were ever to unite and form a nation; no one sect was numerous and strong enough to set up a state church. Americans drifted to the ideals of pluralism because by the time they won their independence they were in fact a pluralistic society. And although thereafter they were never one big happy religious family, religion was no longer a major political issue. They were not seriously distracted by either the interferences of a powerful church or the anticlericalism that split European countries.

Christianity accordingly took on a distinctive American character, which is my reason for devoting a separate chapter to it. First and last, it must be said that the most conspicuous religion of America ever since its founding has been America itself. The sentiment "my country first" that has governed Western history throughout the revolutionary era was here fortified by democratic idealism, pride in "the land of the free." If ordinary patriots were simply boastful, high-minded Americans early came to believe that the supreme mission of the nation was to insure that government of the people, by the people, and for the people should not perish from the earth. Hence the bloody Civil War has been regarded more as a heroic episode than as the national disgrace it was: the main point was that the Union was preserved. Nevertheless, Americans have always considered themselves a religious people. They soon forgot that the founding fathers had pointedly neglected to mention God in their Constitution. They atoned for the neglect by bringing God into their Fourth of July orations and inscribing "In God We Trust" on their coins and dollar bills, possibly their most cherished national emblems. Only such piety raises some questions.

Americans might too easily take their religion for granted, put their real trust in the coins themselves. They might be too content with such formalities as the law recently passed by Congress, putting the nation "under God"—as if Christians could be anywhere else. Even the faith of the high-minded might be too easy, in a land blessed with advantages that the rest of Christendom did not enjoy. My immediate concern is the quality of American religion.

For the sake of perspective, let us consider the first important spiritual movement in the nineteenth century—the diffuse, many-sided affair known as transcendentalism, represented by such writers as Bronson Alcott, Theodore Parker, Margaret Fuller, and above all Ralph Waldo Emerson. Its religious core was the belief in a spiritual reality suffusing all being, especially human beings; God was not transcendent but immanent, not out of this world but through and through it. Transcendentalism accordingly got its name in effect from the human soul, the divine element in man that transcends ordinary experience or ordinary empirical knowledge. The human mind at its highest could know directly the divine mind, or what Emerson called the Over-Soul—the all-embracing, all-infusing spiritual reality.

These ideas were not at all new or original. They owed something to Hindu mysticism, but their major sources were again European. Growing immediately out of Unitarianism, which emphasized the dignity and potential goodness of man, transcendentalism drew its fervor and its more exalted ideas of the possibilities of the human spirit from the Romantic movement, in particular from the German metaphysical idealists, both directly and indirectly, through Coleridge and Carlyle. But again such indebtedness finally accentuated its distinctively American quality. The German idealists and their English pupils settled down as political conservatives, staunch defenders of the traditional aristocratic, authoritarian order. Their American followers were ardent individualists, opposed to tradition and authority, bent on both spiritual pioneering and social reform. Although as individualists they differed among themselves, they were united in an optimistic, democratic faith. Emerson, the foremost Transcendentalist, dwelt most insistently on the divinity in man—every man—and on the thrilling sense of freedom it gave, the wonderful opportunities for new men in a new land and a new age.

Hence he ignored the deterministic implications of pantheism that the more logical Spinoza had insisted on, and ignored as well the logical conclusion of Hindus that individuality is only the mortal element in man, whose immortal soul must be what all men alike share in the World Soul. To Emerson it seemed self-evident that the divinity in man made every man, like God himself, a law unto himself; so his conclusion was his famous gospel of self-reliance. One should always trust to his own inner voice, preserve above all else the integrity of his own mind: "In self-trust all the virtues are comprehended." That society forever demanded conformity only made plainer the corollary: "Whoso would be a man must be a non-conformist." And on these grounds Emerson based his argument for democracy. "Democracy, Freedom, has its root in the sacred truth that every man hath in him the divine Reason, or that, though few men since the creation of the world live according to the dictates of Reason, yet all men are created capable of so doing. That is the equality and the only equality of all men. To this truth we look when we say, Reverence thyself; Be true to thyself."

All this may sound obviously edifying, as it did to the many audiences that applauded Emerson. His gospel was nevertheless revolutionary when taken seriously (as young students in Europe discovered), and it made him a harsh critic of the America of his day. In a land supposedly of rugged individualists and pioneers, he saw everywhere a timid, lazy, slavish conformity, due to a fear both of truth and of public opinion—"the tyranny of democracy." The dignity of man, George Herbert Mead was to say, consists in the fact that when he calls upon himself he finds himself at home; but Emerson complained that most Americans would find nobody home. He attacked the reigning materialism that smothered the divinity in man—the tyranny of business, the worship of property, the hypocrisy and humbug. The God-fearing Puritan had by now pretty well given way to the shrewd Yankee and the Boston merchant, who could be more wholeheartedly devoted to material interests because they continued to go through the motions of religion, while most churchmen were content with formal shows of piety, zealous only in the defense of barren, outworn dogma. The applause usually fell off when Emerson attacked the churches too, and went on to attack dogma itself as a menace to self-trust. "As men's prayers are a disease of the will," he declared, "so are their creeds a disease of the intellect." He rejected the authority of the Bible, especially when it was used to combat new thought and new knowledge. In his fervent hope that a new religion would come out of America he condemned all easy trust, the very heart of its popular religion. "God offers to every mind its choice between truth and repose," he told his fellow Americans. "Take which you please; you can never have both."

Needless to add, most Americans preferred repose. Transcendentalism did not become the religion of America, or inspire any other new one. Its apostles indeed had some apparent influence as crusaders against slavery, and we may well believe that their idealism contributed to the persistence and the vitality of American idealism; among their spiritual children was Walt Whitman. It is worth noting, too, that among their causes was that of women's rights, championed by Margaret Fuller: a cause that Christian churches had neglected for eighteen centuries, and that now aroused their hostility. (The Bible made it quite plain that God had created woman inferior—not to mention all the trouble that Eve had brought on mankind.) Otherwise, so far from effecting a popular spiritual awakening, transcendentalism accentuated a division in American society between intellectuals and common people. This division, natural to all societies, was in the New World due to become a sharper separation, involving more mutual hostility, marked by the characteristic American words "lowbrow" and "highbrow."

Even so, Emerson himself was given to some popular American excesses. At times he located "the divine Reason" in man in the heart, not the head, and in appealing to the heart he indorsed the democratic conceit that common people always have more of it than intellectuals, or use it better. Given his essentially ineffable kind of spiritual truth, he and his fellow Transcendentalists were bound to be vague, always likely to lose themselves in the blue, but they also reflected the national addiction to rhetoric and cloudy generality. As De Tocqueville noted in his *Democracy in America*, the ordinary citizen was very busy with his petty, practical, unpoetic affairs, "habitually engaged in the contemplation of a very puny object: namely, himself"; and whenever he did lift his eyes he saw only the immense images of America, Democracy, Mankind. "His ideas are all either extremely minute and clear or extremely general and vague," concluded De Tocqueville; "what lies between is a void." One may sense such a void in Emerson. Often shrewd and earthy, he may yet seem at the end hazy, abstract, remote from the social and economic realities of American life.[1] But Emerson would come to seem most absent-minded in his optimism, his faith in the wondrous potentialities of man and above all of Americans, in whom he found so few courageous enough to be non-conformists. As his religious vision served mainly to exalt a faith that he already had, so his optimism could gladden men who did not really believe in an immanent God, Over-Soul, or any such highfalutin' spirituality; and it brings up a fundamental issue of religion in America.

Now, today it is easy to ridicule the faith of Emerson. It is much too easy, indeed, and I should say too fashionable in literary circles. His faith in man was not only heartening but basically essential to a faith in democracy, or man's fitness for freedom; for if the traditional emphasis on his natural depravity is better for man's soul, it is not conducive to the cause of freedom. Neither was Emerson being merely absent-minded or inconsistent when he kept hymning the mission of America in the face of all the materialism and the conformism, for he had behind him the most democratic nation of the time, whose achievements were novel enough to kindle imagination, solid enough to warrant hopes for its future. In culture his hopes were being realized by the American renaissance; in social and political life his kind of idealism not only kept America a world symbol of liberty but inspired continual efforts at improvement; and in

[1] For example, he could talk eloquently about love—an odd kind of love "which knows not sex nor person nor partiality." On this John Jay Chapman commented: "If an inhabitant of another planet should visit the earth, he would receive, on the whole, a truer impression of human life by attending an Italian opera than he would by reading Emerson's volumes. He would learn from the Italian opera that there were two sexes; and this, after all, is probably the fact with which the education of such a stranger ought to begin."

74

practical affairs his puny fellow citizens were busy clearing a continent, building a mighty nation. A spirit of optimism stimulated activity in all spheres. Americans remained the most confident of all peoples, at least until the rise of Soviet Russia; and I doubt whether they could maintain their democracy if they ever lost their optimism.

Yet a naïve optimism will no longer do, for either spiritual or political purposes. Those who cling to Emerson's hopes have the more need of realizing that he preached too simple, facile a faith. On religious grounds his doctrine of Compensation is the clue to its inadequacy. In proclaiming his thrilling idea of the divinity of man and nature, he got around the ageless question of whence, then, all the pain and misery, folly and evil, by arguing that such apparent defects in the divine scheme served only to make good possible; sturdily he insisted that all evils were perfectly balanced by the good that came out of them, all virtue was sufficiently rewarded and all wrongdoing sufficiently punished by fear and guilt to make a heaven and hell unnecessary; but he had to insist so much because on earth there clearly is no such "perfect equity." In effect, at any rate, he treated evil as more incidental than fundamental. He denied that there were any really painful mysteries, any tragic dilemmas, any insoluble problems. To the end he kept lecturing Americans on their shortcomings, setting an example of high thinking, but he was likely to edify them by leaving them no more deeply troubled than he himself was. He even objected to the more ardent reformers among the Transcendentalists, who saw no compensation for such very real evils as slavery. "He who aims at progress," said Emerson, "should aim at an infinite, not at a special benefit." High thinking about the infinite could be an escape from hard thinking about economic, social, and political problems.

In this view the Transcendentalists set a complex challenge for the established churches of America. They were critical of conventional dogma, which most Americans accepted unthinkingly; they restated the accepted democratic faith, but were more literal and ardent about it than were most respectable, upper-class churchgoers; they called for fuller self-realization, richer individuality, through the promotion of cultural or spiritual values, in a society that was becoming increasingly devoted to a merely economic individualism and the pursuit of material goods; and they confirmed a popular optimism that was generally shallow and mindless, while it also tended to distract men from the service of God. This was a challenge especially to Protestantism, the dominant religion in America. One can hardly maintain, I think, that the major churches rose to it in the nineteenth century.

The crusade for abolitionism immediately inspired the "Great Revival," in which democratic and Christian idealism were wedded. Thereafter Protestantism bred chiefly religious revivals of the popular kind, wildly emotional but never deep or lasting; when most hysterical they testified that normally Americans felt little sense of sin or need of salvation. Popular preachers included such other types as the Reverend Russell Conwell, who went up and down the land giving his famous lecture "Acres of Diamonds," keynoted by a simplified version of the Protestant ethic: "I say, Get rich, get rich! But get money honestly. . . ." It was apparently the main clause that drew the crowds. Otherwise the churches felt no need of any urgent effort or spiritual renewal to maintain their large following, if only because they in fact had no trouble doing so in a flourishing nation. It was chiefly the liberal sects that lost members, in particular the Unitarians.[2] The major denominations held their own even though their original dogmas were getting blurred, and many or most of their members might have been unable to define and defend the basic theological differences between, say, Methodism and Presbyterianism. They were more complacent because their clergy retained considerable power outside their churches, among other things supplying almost all the college presidents of America (and incidentally maintaining compulsory chapel for students). The most influential leaders were generally disposed to support the business version of Emerson's gospel of self-reliance. President James McCosh of Princeton confirmed the common idea that capitalism was God's plan for man by declaring the divine right of free private acquisitiveness: "God has bestowed upon us certain powers and gifts which no one is at liberty to take from us or to interfere with. All attempt to deprive us of them is theft. Under the same head may be placed all purposes to deprive us of the right to earn property or to use it as we see fit." Politically, Protestantism as a whole identified itself with the interests of the Republican party, which pretty much controlled government until the election of Woodrow Wilson. Progressive movements in America were primarily secular, as they were in Europe.

At the end of the century, however, the social conscience of Protestantism was stirring. The Reverend Charles M. Sheldon published *In His Steps* (1898), in which he proposed a simple method for dealing with social problems—merely to pause and ask the question: What would Jesus do? This possibly excessive simplicity no doubt had much to do with the fabulous success

[2] It should be noted, however, that as a sect appealing to the intelligentsia the Unitarians still wield an influence far out of proportion to their numbers.

of his book, which sold more than 15,000,000 copies; but at least many Americans might discover that Jesus had not urged men to get rich, or preached the God-given right to use property as one saw fit. Sheldon heralded the growing emphasis on the "social gospel" in our century. Outside the South, the churches were now liberalizing their creeds in the light of the "higher criticism" of the Bible and taking to Modernism—a movement that had been much more active in Europe, but was to have a wider and more persistent influence in America. On all counts American Protestantism identified itself most clearly with the modern faith in progress.

But by this time its influence was on the wane. A particular reason was the hordes of immigrants, who settled chiefly in cities; the growth of cities meant a decline in the influence of rural America, always the stronghold of old-time religion. For the same reason the Roman Catholic church was gaining steadily; numbering only some 30,000 members in 1789, at the end of the century it was well on its way to the 43,000,000 it claims today. Its history in America was more distinctive.

In Latin America, where Catholicism was the state religion, the Church earned its government support by supporting the ruling class, the wealthy landowners and military dictators who usually controlled the government. In the United States, where Catholics were a minority sect, they enjoyed full political rights but had to meet the challenge of constant hostility, ranging from militant organized hatred, as in the Know-Nothing party and later the Ku Klux Klan, through the inveterate prejudice of rural Protestantism to the more reasoned suspicion of a church that denied freedom of conscience and seemingly owed its primary allegiance to Rome. Thoughtful Catholics were therefore soon at pains to demonstrate that they were as good Americans

as the members of any other sect. Father Isaac Hecker, founder
of the Paulists, maintained that the authoritarianism of his
church was quite consistent with the political equality and liberty
in which he himself fervently believed. The Catholic hierarchy
was usually much less fervent, in part because it was almost
wholly Irish (as were the political bosses in the cities), and
Irish tradition provided little schooling in either democratic
idealism or political responsibility; but its conservative inclina-
tions were not backed by a strong aristocratic, wealthy class, as
they were in other Catholic countries. The great bulk of American congregations were poor immigrants, who mostly remained
in the working class and naturally tended to be loyal to American democracy. In general, Catholics were relatively unim-
pressed by papal denunciations of the heresies implicit in the
democratic faith. That today they formally subscribe to the
same basic doctrines as their fellows everywhere may obscure
the obvious fact that Catholicism was transformed in the United
States, and became essentially more liberal than it was in either
Europe or Latin America.[3]

A striking instance of Catholic adaptation to American ways
was public education, which, in keeping with tradition, the
clergy at first tended to oppose as a threat to the faith: eventually the Church responded by building the largest system of
Catholic schools in the world. Our century has seen a com-

[3] Catholics themselves often seem unaware of this difference. Many felt
outraged when the Church was abused during the Mexican Revolution in
this century, apparently not knowing that the Mexican Church had long
been allied with a ruling class that battened on privilege and corruption,
while the masses remained miserably poor, and that its wealth and power
stood in the way of democrats who wanted to emancipate and educate the
masses. The small town of Taxco, for example, had supported not only its
magnificent cathedral but a dozen other churches, though it numbered only
a few thousand inhabitants, almost all of them illiterate.

parable growth of Catholic charities, likewise unparalleled in any Catholic country. In the realm of faith, the Church in America condemned the Society of Slaves of the Immaculate Heart of Mary when they declared that the power of grace is restricted to Catholics. For all such reasons, Catholics have in the last generation become politically more respectable, holding more and more public offices that once were almost monopolized by Protestants. (Of two hundred and seven federal judges appointed by Presidents Harding, Coolidge, and Hoover, for example, only eight were Catholics.) Now Protestant America has finally elected a Catholic President. Those who opposed this departure from tradition included many men who had reasoned misgivings; but I assume that today only bigots believe that President Kennedy is any less devoted to democracy because of his religion, or that he is likely to take orders from the Pope. Catholic laymen have also grown more independent, recently protesting against the domination of the clergy, complaining of the many sermons that merely rehearse the routine themes of yesteryear.

Judaism in America has had a comparable history, but with an important difference involving the purer, uglier, prejudice it had to contend with. The millions of poor Jews who emigrated to America hardly needed to be sold democratic ideals of equality and liberty; both the teachings of their great prophets and their long experience of oppression inclined them to a more active concern for social justice. As they prospered they stirred up more active prejudice by acquiring a reputation at once for radicalism and commercialism, or by outshining other Americans in the national game of business; and if only because of such animus they remained as a whole more consistently liberal than either Protestants or Catholics. Meanwhile, however, they too were being changed by the New World, in which at least they enjoyed all the rights of citizenship and did not have to fear pogroms. Many gave up their traditional ways, thinking of themselves first as Americans rather than orthodox Jews. Many turned to Reform Judaism, a liberal version that grew considerably stronger in America than in Europe. A recent neoorthodox reaction illustrates again why deeply religious men may not consider "liberal" simply a good word, for leaders of the movement feel that Judaism was being liberalized to the point of losing its distinctive faith, forgetting its covenant with God; yet they have not reverted to the intransigent orthodoxy that remains a power in Israel itself.

All this is not to say that the religious situation in America today is uniformly cheering. No longer unique as a pluralistic society, America has perhaps more of a religious problem than do most of the Western democracies. There remains plenty of mutual suspicion among the churches, which crops up in such issues as federal aid to education. Secular liberals remain suspicious of all the churches when they try to influence political decisions, or appear to threaten the separation of church and state. Vulgar evangelists continue to aggravate the problems, recalling the muscular Billy Sunday's crusades against "sinners, science, and liberals." Worse, there is still much latent prejudice, which is always likely to flare up in times of crisis or depression. It was not so long ago that the popular Father Coughlin was stirring up anti-Semitism, together with other Fascist sentiments as congenial to the Protestant Ku Klux Klan. In the South, Protestant churches remain the most highly segregated institutions in the country, and Fundamentalist sects produce the most rabid preachers of Protestant white supremacy. Short of such bigotry, studies of public opinion indicate that churchgoers are less favorable to freedom of speech and press than are non-churchgoers.

Nevertheless, America is not seriously torn by either bitter religious strife or bitter anticlericalism. All the major churches support the basic principles of democracy, at least in theory. All are committed to a pluralistic society, taking for granted the existence of other free churches no less when they claim absolute truth for their own doctrines; however disposed to intolerance, none would dare to call for the suppression of their rivals. Secular liberals sometimes welcome the political influence of the churches, now that it is more often exerted on behalf of liberal causes. (I heard no protests from them, for instance, when both Catholic and Protestant clergymen on the West Coast warned their congregations against the John Birch Society.) In spite of all the bigots among us, public debate of religious issues is ordinarily civil—or in view of Western history, one might say extraordinarily civil.

Such civility was admirably exemplified in a recent study, *Religion and American Society*, which went to the heart of the issues that remain concerning the essential quality of American religion. Under the auspices of the Center for the Study of Democratic Institutions, a group of men of different faiths— Protestant, Catholic, Jewish, and humanistic—concentrated on two large questions: what a free society has a right to ask of its religious institutions, and what these institutions have a right to ask of our society. While they naturally differed on every specific issue, they reached some fairly general agreements on basic principles. To my mind, both their agreements and their disagreements were healthy for the purposes of a free society, whose supporters are logically required to believe that diversity of opinion is a good thing, and who now have reason to worry over the growing pressures to conformity or uniformity.

To begin with, the group agreed that religion should not keep aloof from society or the world, and that churchmen should be encouraged to speak out freely on matters affecting public life. Elementary as this policy may seem, it marks a fundamental difference between Judaeo-Christian tradition and Buddhism and Hinduism; for in spite of its otherworldly tendencies Christianity has habitually taken a more active interest in public affairs, including politics. Thereby its churches have also got into considerable trouble, never succeeding in maintaining the hairline distinction of being *in* the world but not *of* it. For a free society a further difficulty is that they have always tended to make absolute assertions about right and wrong, and so far as possible to make them the law of the land; today they still tend to coerce and thereby to curtail personal freedom, Protestants by blue laws and laws against drinking, Catholics by laws against birth control, both by efforts at censorship, and so on. The group also agreed that while religion could best serve American society by acting as its judge, churches should not try to impose their judgments on the whole society by any kind of coercion, or to join the pressure groups on the political scene. Non-believers might add that Americans docilely put up with other strange regulations due to religious tradition, such as laws against suicide; for if men are entitled to life, liberty, and the pursuit of happiness, no right would seem clearer than that of ending one's own life when one is sick of it. I think it fair to say that the consensus of religious America is not clearly rational or consistent, any more than are its political processes.

The sharpest disagreement of the group was over just this question of consensus, specifically whether there ought in fact to be a clear, firm national purpose—what so many men today are saying is the chief need of America. Some maintained that our society rests on principles held to be absolute truths, like those stated in the Declaration of Independence, and that only by holding firmly to this traditional consensus can the nation know and care where it is going, hope to provide world leadership. Others maintained that the essence of a free society is not to be united on goals, and that appeals to allegedly unquestionable truths are dangerous, menacing the right of individuals to pursue their own good, their own truth; or in familiar terms, the consensus is an agreement on the right to disagree peaceably on all first and last questions about God, the good life, and the meaning of man's life. The disagreement accordingly comes down to the problem of the absolute and the relative. Without presuming to settle it, I should again remark that the growth of a pluralistic society suggests a possible consensus on a kind of compromise, perhaps not strictly logical but broadly not unreasonable. We might all agree on the need for integrity, which requires firm principle; to maintain integrity, most men evidently still need to believe that their ethical principles are absolutely right; we may therefore hope that these principles will include a belief in the positive value of a generous, humane, tolerant spirit, a disposition to live and let live; and those of us who are relativists might remember that nevertheless virtually all of us agree that Hitler's extermination of millions of Jews in cold blood was absolutely wrong. Likewise none of us who believe in a free society want any such total community or overriding national purpose as the Communists are dedicated to. As for religion, the issue is somewhat simpler. Most of the churches still claim absolute truth for their basic teachings; in a free society they must have the right to preach the truth as they see it;

but their absolute claims must not be allowed to bind men of different belief, or in effect must be treated as relative.

Otherwise there remain plenty of challenges for the churches of America, a land that dotes on the word "challenge." Among them are the menaces to all spiritual values, or simply to personal dignity, in an ever more commercialized, mechanized society, whose high priests on Madison Avenue are dedicated to the profitable task of maintaining the highest standard of low living in all history. But the primary challenge to the churches, it seems to me, is raised by their popular success. Much of what passes for religious faith in America comes down to a belief that it is simply a good thing to believe—it makes you feel better, maybe makes your neighbor behave better; and it makes no difference what you believe, or how vaguely, so long as you are sincere. I assume that churchmen can be counted on to keep telling Americans that it does make some difference, if only to justify their own denomination; but too many have indorsed the other clauses of this slack, complacent, expedient kind of faith, suited to a society that wants everything made easy, guaranteed, or your money back. Commonly they dwell on the spiritual comforts of religion, the personal satisfaction it gives. They themselves seem complacent simply because most Americans pay lip service to the need for faith, and journalistic champions of the American way (such as *Time* magazine) dress up their devotion to our profit system, or to their advertisers, with prattle about moral and spiritual crusades. They flaunt statistics that indicate a growth in church membership without mentioning the social reasons why many sign up, the concern for status that may produce as many Rotarians or Elks. They disregard polls indicating that most Americans believe they themselves lead

Christian lives—and also believe that most other Americans do not lead such lives.

At least the authors of *Religion and American Society* agreed, too, in deploring the popular uses of religion. They echoed the common complaint of devout men that organized religion is too respectable, too much at home in America, and so too much inclined to abdicate its responsibility as a judge of society. Certainly it has in general demanded little of Americans. To realize how little, one has only to read the prophets of Israel, who also preached at a time of national crisis. Thus the Congress that passed a law putting the nation under God did not thereupon call on Americans to serve God wholeheartedly, or to make any sacrifices whatever; but not many churchmen protested against its tacit assumption that God serves America, God is always in our corner. And too few have remarked the fatuous kind of applause of speakers who denounce the "materialism" of the Russians—applause likely to be followed by a commercial. One may therefore have some misgivings about the devotion of the churches to the American cause in the cold war. Here, I should say, is the supreme challenge they face.

They may be trusted to oppose atheistic communism more solidly than they did fascism and naziism, which at first were not opposed by the Catholic and Lutheran churches. In view of the tyranny of communism, they have good reason to regard the American cause as basically just on both democratic and religious grounds; and they might do much more to rouse Americans from their complacence, their devotion to business and pleasure as usual. At the same time, they cannot afford to regard communism as purely evil; they have to recognize the moral appeal that has made it a world force, stirred a religious kind of fervor, won the support of many Christians. They cannot maintain their spiritual responsibilities by indorsing the popular idea that there is no possibility of compromise with the Communists—an idea that might be right, but if so would almost certainly mean a catastrophic war, possibly the end of Christendom. They cannot afford an uncritical support of the American cause either, even apart from the often doubtful wisdom of American diplomatic policy, the tendencies to a shortsighted opportunism. As judges of their society, they must warn against the dangers of tribalism and chauvinism, the besetting sins of selfishness and above all self-righteousness. Given the American fears of revolutionaries, in a world that will surely go on being revolutionary if it remains a going concern, they might even recall the spirit of Emerson. "If there is any period one would desire to be born in," he wrote, "is it not the age of Revolution; when the old and the new stand side by side and admit of being compared; when the energies of all men are searched by fear and by hope; when the historic glories of the old can be compensated by the rich possibilities of the new era?"

Since I appear to be laying down the law to the churches, I should further emphasize the difficulties they face, due to the very union of religion and democracy in America. Ideally they have a much harder mission than providing answers for a free society in a world crisis: a mission at once to hearten and uplift men, and to guard them against belief in any simple, sure-fire solutions, political or religious—any such false guaranties as communism offers. In this view they cannot be Jeremiahs, prophesying doom to a society still energetic, powerful, and hopeful; but neither dare they support the tradition of mindless, heedless optimism, which panics under pressure and starts men hunting for witches or scapegoats. Then they might recognize further complications. The very vagueness of common religious belief is an aid to consensus, as sharper, firmer beliefs might not be. So is much routine habit, or even apathy. Studies of American communities by James Prothro and Charles Grigg revealed a rather alarming lack of consensus on democratic values, even among the educated; but they also revealed that behavior was more democratic than declared belief—reversing the common assumption about how Americans fall short of their ideals, and suggesting that possibly they are better Christians, too, than their professed beliefs may indicate. The much deplored lack of a clear sense of national purpose may be due in part to a saving spirit of humility, a saving awareness of difficulty.

Still, there is no great virtue or strength in vagueness, sluggishness, or apathy; and I judge that what most needs to be stressed are the dangers of slackness and smugness. Among the heartening signs of the religious revival of recent years was the alarm expressed by some influential churchmen over the popular expressions of this revival. For these hardly look like a spiritual renewal, a real conversion or change of heart. To some extent the popular revival has fed on anxiety, but to a plainer extent it has tended to confirm the easy, self-righteous kind of faith to which Americans were already addicted. The huge sales of Norman Vincent Peale's *The Power of Positive Thinking* suggest chiefly that millions of Americans are religious illiterates, as incapable of a genuine spirituality as of any really hard thinking. I see no more reason for rejoicing in the "Back to God" movement led by the American Legion.

·∻ V ∻·

THE RELIGIOUS REVIVAL

ALTHOUGH RELIGIOUS REVIVALS have been common in Western history, the current one is a heterogeneous affair suited to our confused age, more a drift and sprawl than a definable "movement" like Methodism, Tractarianism, or Trancendentalism. To historians of the future it may accordingly not look like a definite revival, worthy of a name. To me it seems more significant simply because it is nameless, unconcerted, and unlocalized. It has affected not only all the major churches in both Europe and America, but all major cultural interests. In religion proper it appears in the widespread popularity of Thomism, of Kierkegaard and the varieties of Protestant neo-orthodoxy, of such diverse thinkers as Nicolas Berdyaev, Albert Schweitzer, and Martin Buber, and of such other religions as Zen Buddhism. In philosophy its signs include the diverse influences of William James, Bergson, Whitehead, and Jaspers. In literature it has had a number of eminent spokesmen, notably Yeats and T. S. Eliot, by common consent two of the greatest poets of the century. In science it is marked by a more respectful attention to the claims of religion, directly by psychologists, sociologists, and political scientists, ex *cathedra* by some distinguished physicists and biologists. In history the obvious name is Arnold

Toynbee. One cannot be sure, of course, how deep or lasting the consequence of all this thought will be; but the revival has gone on long enough to be viewed as more than a transient fashion. At least one can no longer say easily that "God is dead."

Hence I should at once repeat emphatically that I am not at all impressed by the revival in popular religion, especially in America. The many best sellers on religious themes—tin-pan alley songs, Hollywood films, novels, tracts on the magical power of faith—are almost uniformly shallow when not simply tawdry. Their usual message might be summed up in the statement that there's no better buy than religion: if you only have faith, the Man Upstairs will take care of everything. They accentuate the "religious illiteracy" that now alarms even the optimistic Kenneth Latourette—the common ignorance of the serious claims of religion, or of the commitments entailed by a genuine faith. Certainly they give little indication of anything like a deepening sense of the sacred, a quest for holiness, or a renewed dedication to the service of God. Religious fervor is most apparent in such sects as Jehovah's Witnesses, or in the spasms induced by such evangelists as Billy Graham; and these primitive forms of Christianity can hardly impress one who respects either our knowledge or the teachings of Jesus. They may confirm the suspicion that insofar as the popular revival has had any serious effect this is likely to be a harmful one, another distraction from the tasks of mature thought and responsible behavior.

Otherwise a historical perspective suggests the most that can be said for this revival. Popular religion has never been prone to lofty spirituality, any more in India or medieval Europe than in America today. As Dostoevski's Grand Inquisitor remarked, most men have always sought not God but the miraculous—magical answers to their prayers, or heavenly consolations for all the prayers unanswered. If Americans have less excuse for such demands on God than had the poverty-stricken masses of the past, they still have enough personal problems to keep them prey to anxiety. Piety or simple humanity calls for something of the humility of Nicolas Berdyaev, who himself suffered acutely from "the clash of a passionate love of the world above, of a love of the highest, with pity for this lower world, the world of suffering," and who concluded that the good Christian must realize that among ordinary mortals the spiritual is bound to be reduced to rather low manifestations. Supporters of a free society may then welcome a significant difference between the current religious revival and the religiosity in the last centuries of the Greco-Roman world. The ancient mystery religions flourished on an evident demoralization, a loss of faith in man's own powers, a loss of hope in his earthly future, whereas in spite of their anxieties most Americans are still basically confident of their society. As yet I see no serious signs of a comparable loss of nerve.[1]

I should also discount somewhat the popularity of serious religious writers, like T. S. Eliot and Arnold Toynbee, who have made the cover of *Time* magazine—what has been called the American peerage. This is in part a matter of fashion, what the well-dressed man ought to know or to have on his living-room table. One may suspect that many of their readers have not

[1] I have elsewhere noted the popularity of astrology as an example of the difference. In the Greco-Roman world astrology became a rage in keeping with the growing spirit of fatalism, and then the feverish effort to escape the decrees of fate by magic. In America the many astrologer's columns in the newspapers are sufficiently disgraceful as a sign of vulgar superstition and gullibility in a supposedly educated Christian country, as well as a sign of the routine irresponsibility of newspaper publishers; but they indicate no such spirit of fatalism or serious belief in the stars. They amount to another cheap diversion, like the comics.

really pondered their religious thought, possibly not understood it; or a historian may fear that too many have swallowed Toynbee whole, at one gulp. Similar misgivings may extend to other seemingly respectable manifestations of the religious revival, such as Buchmanism—a movement that looks somewhat too respectable, a classy gospel for good Tories.

Yet I begin with such reservations only to emphasize that many thoughtful people, both in the churches and outside them, are giving more serious attention to religion. Although I cannot know how many, or just what they are thinking, my impression remains that there is a deepening interest, obviously reflecting the crisis of our time, but not to be dismissed as mere anxiety. The many writers who have helped to stir and guide this interest illustrate the usual welter of ambiguous or conflicting tendencies, but for the most part they have not been appealing primarily to fear, nor have they been preaching a simple gospel of salvation. I judge that on the whole modern religious thought has tended to support the interests of a free society. It is in order to validate this judgment that I propose once more to review first its illiberal or dubious tendencies.

The abiding difficulties of a tradition of absolutism are highlighted by the vogue of Thomas Aquinas. Long the official theology of the Catholic church, Thomism grew popular with non-Catholics too in the last generation, for example at the University of Chicago under Robert Hutchins and Mortimer Adler (who inspired the remark that now the Jews were making Catholics out of good Protestants); but its new disciples are likely to accentuate the difficulties for the unconverted. When Jacques Maritain (a former Protestant) claims "scientific certitude" for Aquinas' proofs of the existence of God, argument becomes simply futile; one can only say that he cannot possibly demonstrate this certitude to the satisfaction of many other rational men. No more could Mortimer Adler prove his "axiom" that philosophical knowledge is superior to science because it is an absolutely true knowledge of essential being instead of mere phenomena; and he had an unpleasant way of denouncing his opponents as not only mistaken but irresponsible, almost traitors to the cause of truth—a mode of debate that is not ideally suited to a free society, and recalls that St. Thomas prescribed death for heretics. It may recall, too, a good deal of apparent nonsense in the philosophical knowledge of Aquinas, such as the couple of hundred pages in which he solemnly tells all about angels—their nature, their desires, how they eat and move, etc.

The serious problems arise with the application of supposedly immutable, universal, eternal principles. One has to adapt the thought of Aquinas to our scientific knowledge, based on premises radically different from his Aristotelian premises, and to the needs of a society unlike any that he or Aristotle could ever have imagined.[2] Today an issue of particular consequence is birth control. Logically, the Catholic doctrine of natural law in ethics ought to permit some disagreement over the specific dictates or contents of this law; so one could argue that if God or nature clearly intended sexual intercourse to produce children, nature also sends rain, and people put on raincoats or put up umbrellas anyway. In practice, however, God-given laws are naturally hard to change, and the Church maintains its opposition to birth control; so the upshot is that most educated Catholics practice

[2] Etienne Gilson, the foremost spokesman of Thomism, does not even discuss the questions raised by these outmoded premises in his recent work *The Elements of Christian Philosophy* (New York: Doubleday, 1960). Apparently he takes for granted that Christian philosophy is committed to the philosophy of Aristotle.

it while the poor and ignorant ones in backward countries continue to breed, and to intensify the dangers of the population explosion.

More troublesome is the Protestant reversion to fundamentalism, implicit in the seemingly unorthodox thought of Kierkegaard, and made most explicit by Karl Barth and his many followers in Europe. Barth repudiated the whole effort of Aquinas to make Christianity rational by insisting on not only the absolute but the exclusive authority of the Bible, declaring it the sole source of truth about God and man. Although he admitted that he could not help using the language of philosophy now and then, he did his best to rule out all independent claims of reason, and his more intensely reactionary disciples have spread the idea that philosophy is a bane on religious truth. They have also magnified what to others may seem his quite arbitrary interpretations of the Bible, for instance his neglect of the fact that neither Christ nor the prophets of Israel made any reference whatever to his cardinal doctrine of the fall of man. If his school is no direct menace to religious freedom, it none the less denies the rights of reason or free thought, and its vogue is among the symptoms of the revolt against reason that does seriously menace the free society.

Another such symptom was the popularity of Bergson, due to his celebration of intuition and the *élan vital*. Though he himself attacked primarily the abuses of reason rather than reason itself, his followers joined company with the many who have exalted faith, passion, will, instinct, the heart, and other such faculties or ways of "knowing" that thoughtless or ignorant men may possess abundantly, feel they are better at than are disciplined thinkers, and employ to support whatever they want to believe. And though Bergson has long since gone out of fashion, his influence survives in some thinkers he impressed, notably Carl Jung. "We ought to be particularly grateful to Bergson," Jung declared, "for having broken a lance in defence of the irrational"; and he proceeded to defend it much more systematically. Whereas Freud saw in the unconscious the dark monsters of the irrational, Jung saw in it the oldest, deepest wisdom of the race, in particular the archetypal symbols of religion, which were somehow imbedded in a "racial unconscious." Good Christians might not welcome his restoration of God as a "function of the unconscious," or his recommendation of religion to his patients as a matter of "psychic hygiene," but many writers have been pleased to find in him supposedly scientific authority for the higher, holier truths of poetry, myth, and religion. The trouble remains that almost anything may go on these misty grounds. If the glorification of the unconscious and the irrational may be relatively harmless in surrealism or avant-garde poetry, let us remember that Hitler trusted his intuitions, celebrated the myth, boasted of his scorn of mere reason, stirred up the depths in his people; and what came out was not wisdom.

A different set of symptoms, rather curiously occurring more often in laymen than in theologians, is the tendency to a complete disdain or despair of the modern world. Arnold Toynbee, for one, in his Olympian moods has contemplated quite calmly the probable death of our civilization. Having decided that the only justification for a civilization was the creation of a higher religion, he could see no prospect of our producing one, and therefore no reason why our civilization was worth saving. Likewise the four other civilizations that survive were dying unblessed; in his *Study of History* he concluded that all "are now right out of the picture," thereby washing his hands of two billion human beings. Those in the West might not rejoice at a silver lining he later made out in his clouds, the chance that since we seem doomed to lose most of our economic, social, and political freedom, men might seek compensation in "spiritual freedom"— that traditional kind that even slaves may enjoy. Another historian, Herbert Butterfield, recommended a more positive unconcern in his book *Christianity and History*, which apparently much impressed the university youth of England. Branding as a "disastrous heresy" the faith in human nature on which democracy grew up, Butterfield advised Christians not to take too seriously the struggle between communism and the so-called free world. "Hold to Christ," he concluded, "and for the rest be totally uncommitted." Meanwhile many literary men have been ringing variations on T. S. Eliot's theme that the modern world is a "waste land," in effect maintaining that it quite deserves its doom or damnation, giving it up as hopeless.

Eliot is also a prominent representative of the aristocratic conservatism to which the religious spirit has traditionally been prone. In *The Idea of a Christian Society* he criticized liberalism and democracy as chiefly disorderly or negative movements; the keys to his ideal Christian society are authority and hierarchy, not liberty and equality. In *Notes towards the Definition of Culture* he argued that culture especially requires a privileged class of gentlemen by birth or blood, not an elite selected on the basis of mere ability. While incidentally warning against the influx of "foreign races" and "any large number of free-thinking Jews," he attacked the idea of equality of opportunity, and the effort to approach it through universal education; democratic ideals he declared simply incompatible with the maintenance of high culture. Since he stressed the basic identity of religion and culture, one might remark that he neglected to expound the peculiar religious qualifications of a hereditary privileged class (not to mention the economic system required to support it, the sordid fact that his gentlemen had to be a moneyed class); but in particular Eliot neglected to consider closely the historic record of the privileged aristocracy that dominated Europe for many centuries, and the obvious question whether it had in fact promoted his idea of a Christian society, one "in which the natural end of man—virtue and well-being in community—is acknowledged for all." The most evident reason for the revolutions in the modern world, and now the stir all over the world, is that the common people had cause to believe that their betters were not much concerned about their well-being.[3]

For a high priest of tradition, in short, Eliot lacks the historical sense he prides himself on. This is a common deficiency in religious thinkers, who habitually demonstrate the inadequacy of secular ideals by emphasizing their shortcomings in practice, contrasting them to an ideal Christianity, while disregarding the shortcomings of historic Christianity. It is also symptomatic of a widespread tendency stemming from the Romantic movement (which as a classicist Eliot deplores) to romanticize the religious and aristocratic past, especially the Middle Ages, much as Dostoevski romanticized Holy Russia. Again it comes down to a sentimentality that may not be harmless, for it makes the present seem more intolerable by contrast with an unreal past. It may therefore encourage an evasion of the responsibilities of the present, just as on lower levels the Hollywood gingerbread

---

[3] Another typical example of such oversights is Erik von Kuehnelt-Leddihn, a Catholic monarchist, whose *Liberty or Equality* has won high praise in neoconservative circles. In this he proves, with much flourish of historical reference, that democracy is the main source of modern totalitarianism and tyranny; but he makes no reference to the notorious poverty and misery of many peoples under their Catholic monarchs, or to the fact that dictatorship flourished in Catholic Bavaria, Italy, Spain, Portugal, etc., and has been most vigorously combated by the established democracies.

world tends to unfit its addicts for dealing maturely with their personal problems. Too many literary people lament their fate of having been born in our dreadfully unsettled, vulgar, godless age, which incidentally supports them much more handsomely than medieval society supported Dante, and might remind us that he had a low opinion of his sufficiently unsettled and barbarous age, solacing himself by torturing popes in his *Inferno*.

A related fashion is the current revival of the notion of original sin. This has become so popular a theme that I feel obliged to repeat some elementary observations I have kept making in recent books. Harping on original sin obviously indicates no renewed faith in God but a loss of faith in man, and often it insinuates humiliation rather than real humility. Granted what any sensible person knows, that men are naturally inclined to be selfish and frail, I do not think it clarifies matters to give their unoriginal sins this name. Instead it tends to obscure the historical fact that the doctrine of original sin was for many centuries a basic argument for the subjection of the common people, as it was for serfdom and slavery, and that democracy rose only when the doctrine was questioned, and more faith in ordinary human nature was declared. It may obscure the logical necessity of such faith for a free society; for if this has plainly been too optimistic a faith, possibly the "disastrous heresy" that Herbert Butterfield called it, there can be no hope for a free society unless men are good enough to be trusted with the rights and liberties that neither the medieval church nor the Protestant reformers saw fit to grant them, and that the leaders of the Soviet also deny them. I think that Reinhold Niebuhr, among others, has undermined his political liberalism more than he realized or intended by his insistence on the natural depravity of man.

Niebuhr, however, recalls us to the positive values of the

religious revival for the purposes of a free society. Like him, most of the leading Protestant thinkers have been devoted to these purposes. Karl Barth himself preached an uncompromising opposition to political tyranny, and his followers in Germany were among the first actively to resist Hitler. Likewise, some of the most influential Thomists have been political liberals, notably Jacques Maritain, a leader of the democratic movement among French Catholics. If Aquinas hardly anticipated or wanted a political society such as ours, much of his thought can support its basic principles; and his whole monumental effort at a rational theology—in its day a daring "modernist" theology, involving an effort to embrace the heretical science of Aristotle—may still inspire resistance to rigid conservatism, as to any blind faith. Another Catholic writer lately grown popular is Lord Acton, who has inspired something of a cult in England. Although his admirers seem drawn to him more as a deeply religious historian than as an ardent liberal, his passion for liberty is in any case spread all over his work. And his resolute insistence on maintaining pure Christian standards of historical judgment—the reason for his endless unhappiness over the historic record of his Church—brings up the most obvious reasons why democrats may welcome the support of religion. These are teachings at once so commonplace and so notoriously violated that sophisticates may underrate their importance.

Simplest of all is the gospel of charity or love. The spirit of love is pretty rare in revolutionaries; it is not overly conspicuous in most reformers or professional agents of social welfare, and let us add at once that it does not radiate from most sermons, theological discourses, or literary portraits of the Christian society; yet it does inform much of the religious literature of our time.

It is associated with other simple ideas that have helped to make a world of difference in Western history, notably the idea of the sacredness of the person, a basis for his claims to rights not commonly enjoyed in other societies. (How much difference this might make was brought home to me in a discussion with some Japanese professors, who had just begun to realize that the idea was lacking in their own tradition. One reported in dismay that when he tried to persuade his class that the Japanese tradition of political assassination was deplorable, finally noting that it was just wrong to murder people, his students looked blank: they asked *why* it was wrong.) A related expression of the same spirit is Albert Schweitzer's gospel of reverence for life. As he observed, the reverence implicit in Christian teaching helps to explain why there has been much more indignation over social injustice in the Western world than in historic India, whose holy men typically preached non-attachment to the temporal world and could therefore be unconcerned about the earthly miseries of the Hindu masses. It also illumines an essential difference between America and the Soviet that many European and Asiatic intellectuals overlook. America is indeed materialistic, it can be as hypocritical and self-righteous as Russia in its diplomacy, and unquestionably it operates on the same dangerous principle that the end justifies the means; yet it is not purely Machiavellian on principle, it plays power politics with an uneasy conscience, always stirring up much open protest at home, and as unquestionably it shows more respect for the rights of men, the avowed moral ends of democracy.

In the last generation or so the Christian concern with social and political problems has grown deeper and livelier than ever before. Although there has never been better reason for fearing the end of man's world, none of the prominent leaders of the

2.1745

religious revival are returning to the otherworldly tradition of Christianity, none are preaching the way of saintly or mystical withdrawal from earthly interests. In this respect Karl Barth is no reactionary: he called for active Christian charity in social life, on behalf of the working classes, and is now as concerned over the state of culture. Arnold Toynbee has not really withdrawn either; since completing his universal history for posterity he has pitched in and tried to help keep our civilization going, even though it still gives no promise of siring a higher religion.[4] There is little likelihood, I take it, that many churchmen or laymen will follow Herbert Butterfield's advice to remain wholly uncommitted to all but Christ; and I suspect that Butterfield himself is committed strongly enough to the values of a free society.

For our immediate purposes such relative simplicities may well be most important. There remain, however, some significant developments in religious thought that might count for more in the long run. In general they are further developments of Modernism or liberalism, which neo-orthodox theologians have sharply criticized but have supplemented rather than repudiated. In particular they reflect a growth of historical-mindedness and social awareness, a fuller consciousness of the paradoxes or ambiguities of religious faith, and a deeper sense of complexity and difficulty, involving some admission of ultimate uncertainty. They may therefore seem unwholesome to many devout men, who may doubt that this is the way to religious conversion or a genuine faith; and so far as I can see, the religious revival has not in fact led to any such wide or deep con-

---

[4] I am pleased to add that he recently upset some of his journalistic admirers by attacking Madison Avenue as the most serious internal menace to the American cause. Roy Larsen of *Time* magazine felt impelled to spring to the defense of his advertisers.

version as early Christianity did. What I make out is more a growing interest and disposition to believe than a full commitment or whole-hearted belief. But I assume that to remain vital, religion must adapt itself to the conditions of a revolutionary world, for better or worse, and that its concessions to modern knowledge and modern thought are at least better for the purposes of a free society.

On this assumption I should now pay some tribute to the thought I reviewed unfavorably. T. S. Eliot's criticism of democratic culture is clearly pertinent and often acute; at his best he exemplifies the value and the need of the conservative philosophy which John Stuart Mill recognized in Burke and Coleridge, that it recalls truths that ordinary conservatives have forgotten and too many liberals have never known. Sober rationalists may likewise respect the attack of Bergson on rationalism, or at least the grounds on which it began. William James joined him in rebelling immediately against the reign of a narrow, rigid positivism, which still saddles much contemporary thought. This too easily discredits basic human interests and values, including ideals of justice and freedom, by limiting significant meaning to scientific truth, dismissing as meaningless or false what strictly is merely unverifiable. It not only blasts the claims of religion but menaces the claims of all the liberal arts, drastically reduces the scope of philosophy, and may impede science itself, especially the sciences of man. James remarked that scientists tend to rule out all the "wild data" that do not fit into their scheme—the kind of data that Freud was then investigating, and thereby incurring the hostility of both positivists and churchmen. James himself nevertheless impressed many European thinkers (including the great sociologist Max Weber) by his classic study *The Varieties of Religious Experi-*

ence, in which he treated such experience as a scientific reality, to be explained instead of explained away.

The work of Jung was accordingly no mere aberration. He knew more about religion than did Freud, whose inveterate hostility to it sprang from too simple a view of it as mere wishful thinking. One need not believe in Jung's archetypes imbedded in a racial unconscious to agree that he unearthed very ancient symbols and archetypal myths deeply imbedded in our own tradition, common to many diverse cultures, and corresponding to basic human interests and needs. Paul Tillich accepts his criticism of the Protestant disposition to "iconoclasm," or the destruction of essential religious symbols, which have been confused with incidental forms or accidental signs. Short of Jung's celebrations of the irrational, most unbelievers might agree as well that man cannot live on reason alone any more than bread alone, and that wisdom requires respect for needs so old and deep, needs which rationalists have too often dismissed as primitive or merely neurotic.

To my mind, however, William James remains the best representative of this whole critique. As a pragmatist he discounted the pretensions of "pure" reason in order to establish a fuller confidence in the legitimate claims of reason, but above all he wanted to keep horizons open. Despite his own intense experience of *Angst*, he retained an adventurous spirit, the kind of spirit that Whitehead emphasized was suited alike to science, to religion viewed as spiritual quest, and to the needs of a free society in a revolutionary world. In arguing for the right to religious belief, James did full justice to the scientific spirit that made many men distrust such belief because of insufficient evidence, but he pointed out that men had to commit themselves to some living faith, and could never base it on really conclusive evidence. He noted as truly that there is no scientific or any other method for steering safely between the opposite dangers of believing too little and too much; and while he knew that most men are always inclined to believe too much, too easily, he observed that the scientifically minded might miss possible truth because of a squeamish fear of possible error. Today we all know the type of sophisticate, or semisophisticated "realist," who is ever fearful of being duped or taken in, and so is suspicious of all avowed idealism. (He begins as the sophomore who knows that love is nothing but a biological urge to reproduce the species—even though he is least interested in reproduction when he has a purely lustful animal eye on a girl.)

James also pointed to religious possibilities that may seem strange or offensive to the orthodox, but that pervade much modern thought and make for openness. What he believed in was not the omnipotent, omniscient God of Judaeo-Christianity but a deity somehow limited, a power of good that does not have things all its own way, or that he was content to call simply "the ideal tendency in things." If this left open the crucial question where all the evil or un-ideal tendencies come from, one might remark that the orthodox answer of a Satan deliberately created by a self-sufficient God is not wholly satisfying either; but in any case James characteristically did not pretend to certainty or finality. Other thinkers have found his "ideal tendency" in the cosmos revealed by modern science, which may look grander as well as more mysterious than the cozier world envisaged by Christians in the past. Bergson's theory of creative evolution remains unacceptable to biologists, who can make nothing of his *élan vital* except a fancy baptismal formula, and who see no such purposefulness in natural selection working on random variations; but at least Bergson pointed to a positive, ideal aspect of an evolution that did, after all, produce the human spirit—a consciousness of the mighty process. Lately this has inspired Julian Huxley's gospel of evolutionary humanism. Huxley in turn has contributed to the current excitement over the work of the Jesuit Pierre Teilhard de Chardin, who was both mystic and man of science, and who arrived at a new vision of God by an extrapolation of the theory of evolution. Teilhard suggested that the meaning of man's history was not revealed once and for all by Christ, but that evolution has yet to reach its goals.

Social scientists have likewise given religion more intellectual prestige, as well as more headaches, by serious, often sympathetic studies of it. Thus Durkheim treated it as a fundamental social reality, concluding that it was the very origin of the social sense of solidarity. Anthropologists and students of comparative religion have revealed connections between Christianity and prehistoric religion, which again may distress the orthodox but would seem becoming to a religion that claims universality. Toynbee has drawn heavily on all such studies—a vast amount of knowledge that was not available to Lord Acton, who may therefore look parochial by contrast. As one who does not trust Toynbee much as either historian or prophet, I should now acknowledge the values of breadth and catholicity in his treatment of religion. Although he started his Study of History on the seemingly arbitrary premise that the Christian God was the one true God, in mid-career he decided that Christianity was on a par with other higher religions, all of which offer only dim, partial visions of "Absolute Reality," and that any claims to a monopoly on religious truth were as blasphemous as they were preposterous. His continued prestige in America is among the many evidences of a more hospitable, tolerant religious spirit in this century, a spirit clearly essential to better understanding in the effort at world order and peace. Father Walter Ong has reminded Catholics that the problem of pluralism and coexistence is actually a very old one, which was obscured by the provinciality of medieval Europe and the romantic idea of it as a self-sufficient, entirely integrated "Christendom."

Toynbee also belongs to the growing company of writers who are stressing that Westerners can learn much from the great Eastern religions, especially about the "spiritual freedom" or peace of mind that many now yearn for. Religious thinkers who remain closer to home are indeed given a profound pessimism, which is in part an extreme reaction against the faith in progress, a possibly morbid suspicion of any optimism about man. But at its most profound this pessimism springs from a tragic sense of history lacking in Toynbee, despite his preoccupation with the breakdown, decline, and death of civilizations. It is truer to a religious tradition that has taken history seriously, and has not made serenity the supreme goal. As represented by Reinhold Niebuhr, the best-known theologian in America today, it seems to me a more pertinent contribution of the religious spirit to a free society in a state of crisis.

Niebuhr's thought harks back to Kierkegaard, who had been virtually unknown in America before the thirties, and whom he introduced to theological students. It became more tense as the world crisis became more acute, deepening both his conviction of the necessity of resisting the tyranny of totalitarianism and his fear of the habitual complacence of the democracies. By the same token he appears wiser as well as more humane than Kierkegaard. His thought is much more comprehensive, grounded on as much more historical and social sense; he is more thoroughly, consistently aware of paradox, the absurd mixture of good and evil in man that as he sees it makes democracy both possible and necessary; he makes no such fetish of despair and *Angst*, but keeps both his head and his heart. If his popularity owes a good deal to the vogue of original sin, he nevertheless speaks for a liberal faith, religious and political, which may be more wholesome and convincing because it is tough-minded.

Specifically, Niebuhr's possible overemphasis on the radical evil in man springs from a keen awareness of both the shallow optimism of historic liberalism and the spiritual arrogance of historic Christianity. Liberals and churchmen alike succumbed to the besetting sins of pride and self-righteousness because they were alike blind to the tragic ironies of history, due to the paradoxical nature of man: a creature of history who is at once capable of freedom and bound by necessity, who forever seeks the infinite and eternal, and who forever remains finite and fallible. Niebuhr therefore condemns all pretensions to absolute certainty and finality, and freely admits the historical relativism that other religious thinkers deplore. Within this world, he insists, there is "no historical reality, whether it be church or government, whether it be the reason of wise men or specialists, which is not involved in the flux and relativity of human existence, which is not subject to error and sin, and which is not tempted to exaggerate its errors and sins." Religion so often confuses political life and endangers democracy "precisely because it introduces absolutes into the realm of relative values." In his view the ideal contribution of Christianity to democracy is "the spirit of humility" required by the necessities of co-operation and compromise.

Finally Niebuhr leads us to another thinker he helped to introduce to America—Paul Tillich. By general consent the most important Protestant theologian of our time, Tillich serves best to sum up and round out this chapter in religious history because he has been most intensely concerned with the relations of religion to society and culture, and has made the most comprehensive, thoroughgoing response to the challenge of the world crisis. This he regards as a more profound challenge to Christianity than other religious thinkers admit. He believes that the traditional message of neither Catholicism nor Protestantism will suffice; he calls for radical self-criticism by all the churches, as by all believers in a free society. He feels no assurance that Protestantism will rise to the challenge, or that any substantial group will take up what he considers its ideal message—one that supports human dignity and freedom, but offers no guaranties. His book *The Protestant Era* ends with a question, whether this era is not ending. Not to mention the possible ending of history itself, about which he believes the Christian message has nothing to say.

These issues I shall consider in my concluding chapter, which will likewise end with questions; for I assume that uncertainty about the future is not only an imperious fact but a necessary condition of man's actual freedom. Here I should add that by Tillich's standards of judgment my survey of the religious revival has probably been too cheerful, too favorable to religion. Certainly it is not clear that the churches have taken a permanent new lease on life, or that churchmen in general are engaged in self-criticism as radical as Tillich deems necessary. More apparent are the signs of religion being conducted at the same

old stand, in what may often seem an absent-minded spirit.[5]
At the moment there are also signs of a revulsion against the
"social gospel," or an apparent retreat to safer positions. Nevertheless, the spirit of self-criticism is abroad. We may disagree
about its value or its necessity to religious faith; but I think it
has clearly gone wide and deep enough to be reckoned with.

[5] Governor Rockefeller, for instance, publicly went on record with this
statement: "Knowledge is of value only insofar as it is in accord with the
spiritual truths inherent in our Judaeo-Christian tradition." One may doubt
that practical Americans who felt edified by his remark really believe it, or
that he himself does either.

⊹ VI ⊱

THE CHALLENGE OF THE WORLD CRISIS

Having so far maintained, I hope, a decent appearance of objective historical survey, I now come to the highly debatable issues of the hour; so I should say plainly once more that no man can be utterly objective in these vital matters, my judgments have been debatable all along, and from here on my fallibility will be only more apparent. While my primary concern remains the issues of a free society, these have been further complicated because history has moved on to a world stage, for the first time has become literally universal history. Christianity and democracy no longer contend or join forces in their own private theater alone; both are implicated in a world drama, in which other religious and secular faiths are playing a part, and the fate of the whole human race is at stake. My hope remains that by a historical perspective one may attain at least a measure of detachment, and size up somewhat more adequately the awesome challenge to both. And, let us at once add, their opportunity: for Christianity and democracy have alike been missionary gospels proclaiming universal ideals, declaring the duties or the rights of mankind. Now they have a chance to prove themselves in a universal arena.

The Christian churches have already responded by efforts to

unite. Some 170 churches are represented in the World Council of Churches, set up in 1948, which after many years of debate made a start toward overcoming the problem stated by an Anglican bishop: "The great and terrible difficulty is that the churches cannot unite unless they are willing to die." So far they have managed to co-operate by requiring only a minimum faith in Christ as God and Savior, otherwise blurring their differences by suitably broad or ambiguous pronouncements. At the moment the Second Vatican Council has met to reconsider the role of the Catholic church in the contemporary world, and the possibility of reconciliation with the Protestant and Orthodox churches—with fellow-Christians who only a generation ago were commonly described as "heretics" or "schismatics," and who now are given the gentler name of "separated brethren." Many prelates wish to modernize or liberalize the teaching of the Church, some even to affirm the right of all men to worship God as they believe.

I venture the doubt, however, that any union with the separated brethren will be achieved in the foreseeable future. At least the Roman church gives little sign of willingness to surrender its claim to infallibility in matters of faith and morals, still less of willingness to die; as avowedly the only true church of Jesus Christ, it may be called strictly the least catholic of the major churches. Protestants can hardly accept its terms without surrendering their own fundamental principles. As it is, the Roman church forces a basic religious issue for modern man.

It has certain clear advantages, beginning with the longest unbroken tradition of authority. In Thomism it has the most comprehensive system of theology and ethics, which as a supranaturalistic system is theoretically applicable to every society.

At the same time it has traditionally managed, however belatedly, to adapt its static, immutable principles to changing conditions, as in this century it has accommodated itself to democracy. Above all, it offers men absolute certitude, and so might serve their deepest need in a revolutionary age. Carl Jung, who believed that the ultimate problem of the many hundreds of patients he treated was finding a religious outlook on life, reported that most of these patients were Protestants, only five or six were believing Catholics. Given the deep confusions, uncertainties, and anxieties of our time, Catholic thinkers might say, "I told you so." Others might add, more unhappily, that maybe Dostoevski's Grand Inquisitor was right—men are unable to endure freedom from "miracle, mystery, and authority." If our civilization is disintegrating, the Roman church might again become the main hope of salvation, as it did in the crumbling Greco-Roman world.

Still, this is also to intimate that it might not save our civilization, any more than it did the Roman Empire. Meanwhile Catholicism has only been holding its own; it has not been gaining at the expense of Protestantism or other religions. The problem remains that most thoughtful men are simply unable to believe in its absolute truths, the infallible authority of its church, or the miracle of its sacraments. Paul Tillich therefore asserts that it does not take seriously enough the situation of modern man, or in particular the world crisis; if it is maintaining its integrity by refusing to compromise on its basic dogmas, in another aspect it may appear irresponsible by "presuming to possess a human guaranty against the ultimate threat to everything human." At any rate, it is meeting the threat of disintegration in the authoritarian manner of the political dictatorships. In a more logical world it might be allied with communism, which does not logically have to be godless. Jacques Maritain suggested that the Soviet of the future conceivably might denounce atheism as another form of bourgeois decadence; and if so, the Roman church conceivably might accommodate itself to the system, as it did to Mussolini's fascism, and as the Russian Orthodox church has managed to do.

By contrast, Tillich recognizes the evident appeal of the authoritarian principle—Catholic, Communist, or National Socialist—in the efforts at mass organization or reintegration; yet he holds as uncompromisingly to the basic principle of Protestantism, the refusal to accept the absolute claims of any human authority. The striking fact, he remarks, is that in an age of anxiety the influence of the Catholic church is not more powerful than it is. And though one may nevertheless have doubts about the adequacy and the validity of his own religious message, I propose to consider it at some length as a message that is more clearly suited to the conditions of modern thought and knowledge, and to the needs of a free society.

Unlike Karl Barth, Tillich holds that the Protestant principle now requires a surrender of its historic appeal to the Bible as a source of infallible truth, since we know that the Bible is a human document, containing much mythical and legendary material. While he stresses the need for myths as religious symbols, he stresses as much the danger of mistaking them for literal truth. Similarly he insists on the danger of attacks on the claims of reason, as at once a violation of humanity and a corruption of faith. Faith he defines as "the state of being ultimately concerned," committed to the ultimate—not as any literal belief; it calls for no sacrifice of intellect, of our historical knowledge, or of philosophy or science. He upholds not only the value but the need of doubt, an "existential doubt"; for faith is necessarily a risk, man is always separated from the divine, he can never completely comprehend the ultimate to which he is committed. Altogether, Tillich rejects both spiritual and political totalitarianism precisely for the sake of wholeness. "Ultimate concern," he declares, "is related to all sides of reality and to all sides of the human personality"; and all authoritarian gospels are partial and exclusive when not tyrannical.

Hence he disagrees too with the conventional religious critics of our secular culture, who tend to regard the secular as not merely non-sacred but essentially irreligious. Tillich rejects the seductive medieval ideal of a culture unified and dominated by religion, because this naturally imposes narrow standards, restricts both rationality and creativity. He proposes instead the ideal of a "theonomous" culture, one whose creations are suffused by an ultimate concern but are not necessarily expressed in specifically religious terms. On these grounds he can join T. S. Eliot and others in deploring a purely autonomous culture that encourages a shallow, crude materialism, and makes business its most serious concern. Unlike Eliot, he can appreciate the religious quality of the humanistic tradition coming down from the Renaissance and the Enlightenment. He emphasizes not only the naturalness but the necessity of secularism for religious purposes as well, on the grounds that Protestantism "by its very nature demands a secular reality." It demands "a concrete protest against the sacred sphere and against ecclesiastical pride," a constant spur to the radical self-criticism that the churches are always disposed to shirk or resist. It cannot call for any such special philosophy or ethic as Catholicism has sanctified, and Thomists still argue is essential. Today it calls rather for a religious spirit as bold and adventurous as that displayed in modern science and art.

In particular Tillich discounts the clichés about the loss of faith in the modern world. Faith as an ultimate, unconditional concern is plain enough in communism; he recognizes the spiritual power of the enemy, which is too often obscured by the loose or smug talk about the materialism of the Soviet. He recognizes as well the power of a purely humanistic faith, dismissed by too many religious thinkers—including Niebuhr—as necessarily inadequate. He therefore qualifies the popular thesis that democracy can be maintained only on the spiritual basis of Christianity, a thesis that can be dangerously misleading and divisive even apart from its abuse by such organizations as the American Legion. He knows that the Christian faith is not clearly essential for democratic idealism, and that on the record it has been still less clearly the main driving force behind such idealism. Just because he believes that Christianity can contribute a great deal by its ideal concern for the person, he has dwelt on the historic failure of both Protestantism and Catholicism to develop a sufficient concern for the person in the working class.

Above all, Tillich takes history with the utmost seriousness. He summons Christians to a full consciousness of history and to an "existential concern" with it, a much tenser concern than most historians evince. He warns against the natural tendency of the religious spirit to seek refuge from the temporal in eternity; like the prophets of Israel, he believes that salvation for the community must be in and through history, not *from* history. He warns too against the religious conservatism that regards the establishment of the Christian church as the decisive or even the "final event," the key to the essential meaning of history, and that therefore forbids any radical criticism of the church (just as political conservatives idolize some past event, and like that group curiously named the Daughters of the American Revolution, "try to prevent forever any kind of revolution in the future"). Christians have yet to learn the plainest lesson of history, that the churches have always consecrated some particular temporal order or ideology, in effect committed themselves to idolatry, in order to support their worldly interests. As medieval Catholicism blessed the feudal order, so Protestantism came to bless the bourgeois order, likewise without a serious, sustained effort to judge or transform it. It is for such reasons that Tillich said the first word to be spoken by religion today must be a word against religion.

The next word, however, is much harder. Faith is ideally an unconditional commitment to an ultimate concern; yet the plainest conditions of human history are flux, relativity, contingency, ultimate uncertainty. So Tillich must ask and does ask: What then is truth? Immediately, in everyday life: Can the unconditional claim with which every moral demand imposes itself on human conscience be maintained if the contents of the demand are different in every period of history? Beyond this difficulty loom the larger questions raised by a revolutionary world. Looking back, we can make out epochal turning points, or what Tillich likes to call a *kairos*, "the right time" for momentous change, such as early Christians made out in the message of Jesus. He believes that the movement most conscious of such a *kairos* in our time is religious socialism, and he looks forward to a "new theonomous age" in which religion and secular culture will no longer be alienated. Still, we are bound to ask: May not the message of the *kairos* be wrong? His immediate answer is Yes: history shows that the message "is always an error," in that the imminent ideal is never really fulfilled, the Kingdom of God or the classless society is never at hand.

Worse, something new and terrible has lately come into history —the real possibility of "the end." It may be that the prophets of doom are the true prophets, what is at hand is the final catastrophe. And so the ultimate question is forced: What is the meaning of man's history? A history that until lately Christians had come to believe was a progress, but that has always been spelled by catastrophe, shrouded by painful mystery, and that now may be coming to an end?

Tillich cannot answer any of these questions, of course, by invoking any absolute authority such as Christians have always fallen back on. Neither does he resort to a tactic common to religious thinkers today, who triumphantly point to the final uncertainty of our empirical knowledge in order to assert or imply the superior certainty of religious truth—which strikes me as about the last word in *non sequitur's*. But he draws on other resources of the Christian faith that are more available to men of different faiths, and that may make perhaps the strongest case for the value of religion in a world in crisis. Without denying the historical relativity of values, he manages to find an absolute in the principle of love. Love serves him better precisely because of the ambiguity he sees in it, as being itself a kind of law prescribed by Christ that is nevertheless above all law, religious or political, written in holy scriptures or constitutions. "*Love alone*," he affirms, "*can transform itself according to the concrete demands of every individual and social situation without losing its eternity and dignity and unconditional validity.*" Let us add that this principle never tells us just how to go about expressing our love, or just what to do about the inescapable problem of conflicting loyalties or loves, in a world peopled by many unlovable types and some hateful ones; but translate the principle into simple good will, such as we meet and count on every day, and we may realize that an awareness of relativity is not in fact a dreadful strain on conscience; usually we have little trouble deciding what is the right or decent thing to do, and perplexity itself is a sign of a live moral sense, better for a free society than unthinking obedience to convention or command. Throughout history, C. P. Snow observed, "far more, and far more hideous crimes, have been committed in the name of obedience than in the name of rebellion."

As for this bloody history, Tillich's primary message is that it *does* have some transcendent, ultimate, eternal meaning, symbolized by Jesus as the Christ. Needless to add, this is no utopian meaning, no assurance of endless progress on earth, no denial of the endless tragedy in history. It demands of the Christian that he be at once *in* history and *above* it. Above it he must cling to what Tillich calls the "religious reservation," the attitude of "in spite of"; faith declares an eternal meaning in spite of "the tragic destiny of all human truth and goodness" on earth. In history he must be loyal to the "religious obligation" or the attitude of "because of," the unconditional demand that he keep striving to realize truth and goodness; he must devote himself with "absolute seriousness" to earthly aims that he knows are "fragmentary and ambiguous." Tillich translates the original Protestant doctrine of justification by faith into a radical proclamation of the human "boundary-situation," the limits of possibility on earth, best symbolized by the Cross. Men have always been crossed by inescapable uncertainty and insecurity, the menace of despair, which they have commonly tried to escape by sacrament and priestcraft, magical or mystical union with the divine; but their only hope of real assurance lies in accepting their situation and giving up all illusion of security. And today they must face up to the ultimate threat to human existence, the possible end of history.

Tillich's "boundary-situation" accordingly amounts to a restatement of Kierkegaard's existentialist doctrine of *Angst,* or the universal experience of despair. His message is as remote, I should say, from the gospel of the historic Jesus, who seemed not at all uncertain about the Kingdom of God or the way to salvation. But he is obviously closer to the spirit of Jesus in his concern for the salvation of the community, the "crowd" that Kierkegaard disdained as untruth; while he is also more realistic in recognizing that thoughtful men today cannot be required first to accept theological truths, even about Christ. He never blinks the essential uncertainty and insecurity that Kierkegaard might too easily evade in spite of all his fear and trembling, since his faith was guaranteed by the God of Abraham, the unquestioned authority of the Bible. By the same token, Tillich proclaims the need of openness to all new possibility, in both religious and secular culture. More fully aware of both the values and the costs of human freedom, he more courageously assumes its risks. Despite a more tragic vision of human history, including Dostoevski's awareness of the demonic element in man, he therefore expresses more hope for man. Having declared that the message of the *kairos* is always in error, he adds that it is always right too; for those who proclaim that a new time is coming reveal that the ideal is already there, a present reality, a power that is affecting the future. As he sees it, the "religious reservation" and the "religious obligation" unite in hope, which should be the ultimate word of religion to men today.

As I see it, many men in the free world might do better with such hope, wrung from so unflinchingly realistic a view of the precariousness of the human situation. Behind the many signs of anxiety lie the basic contradictions of the modern world: the common feeling of impotence in a massive civilization endowed with immense power, the common hollowness or emptiness of life amid an unprecedented affluence, the common lack of clear or high purpose in ceaseless activity backed by terrific energy and drive, the common appearances of a flight from freedom. The most thoughtful men outside the churches who still assume the responsibilities of selfhood have to contend with more deeply troublesome threats to integrity and wholeheartedness. They now know that science is no sure way to final truth, any more than to wisdom or goodness; they can no longer hold to any simple faith in progress; and as many became disillusioned with secular religions such as Marxism, they learned to distrust all ideologies, any white hope in revolution or reaction. Today, in view of the possibility of final catastrophe, they may realize that the question of the "meaning" of history is not an academic one, or so pointless as positivists have asserted. They may be oppressed by the apparent meaninglessness of man's whole history. Lord Balfour's account of the final extinction of all life on earth, which science has long predicted is certain, may now seem more poignant:

> The energies of our system will decay, the glory of the sun will be dimmed, and the earth, tideless and inert, will no longer tolerate the race which has for a moment disturbed its solitude. Man will go down into the pit, and all his thoughts will perish. The uneasy consciousness which in this obscure corner has for a brief space broken the contented silence of the universe, will be at rest. Matter will know itself no longer. "Imperishable monuments" and "immortal deeds," death itself, and love stronger than death, will be as if they had not been. Nor will anything that is, be better or worse for all that the labor, genius, devotion, and suffering of man have striven through countless ages to effect.

Or as Santayana added, the one enduring result of all man's works is that the earth may cast a slightly different shadow on the moon. So Tillich argues that only a belief in an "eternal Presence" can assure us that mankind has not existed in vain.

There remains, however, the obvious question, whether his own faith is valid and adequate. First I should say that in spite of his generous appreciation of different faiths, including purely humanistic ones, Tillich tends at once to exaggerate and to slight somewhat the difficulties of unbelievers. Periodically he reverts to the conventional argument that "only" the Eternal can suffice for man, only the paradoxical grace of God can save a being who is necessarily estranged from God. Actually many men, today as in the past, feel no need of such supernatural assurances and manage to carry on decently and responsibly without them, to feel at home in the natural world; just as whole societies, like those of classical Greece and Confucian China, managed to make a reputable history without believing that human history had a transcendent, eternal meaning. In any case, many men of good will are no longer able to believe in God, and in simple humility may doubt that so finite, fallible a mortal as man must be insured by the infinite. Granted that any living faith is necessarily a leap beyond the truths known by reason, men may still want to look before they leap (even if he who hesitates may be lost) because they know that leapers can land almost anywhere, and they still need to believe that their faith is in some sense *true*. Tillich is not very helpful in the crucial decision of what faith to choose, on what grounds. When he declares, for instance, that "The truth of faith consists in true symbols concerning the ultimate," or adequate expressions of the "really ultimate," he leaves us on pretty hazy grounds. One who respects his own symbol of Christ may still

suspect that choices in the "really ultimate" come down to cultural choices, due to temporal accidents of birth, and that their
adequacy might involve some wishful thinking.

Within religion the question remains whether Tillich's kind
of ideal faith can take hold, even though he offers it on lenient
doctrinal terms. In concluding his *Protestant Era*, he wrote that
men who agreed on its essential principles need not belong to a
Protestant or even a Christian church, but he did not appear
confident of the prospects of such a new reformation. He recognized that the Protestant churches were tending to meet the
challenge of authoritarianism by going on the defensive, falling
back on the authority of their own dogma, often with the aid of
more stress on ritual and sacrament. So far as I can see, quite a
few churchmen have been moving toward Tillich, but most of
them have stopped well short of his radical insistence on uncertainty and insecurity, or the "human boundary-situation." And if
they are not responding boldly enough to the world crisis, as
churchmen they have, once more, some plain excuse.

What most men seek—insofar as they are seeking—is most
obviously spiritual security and certainty. Although as a theologian Tillich usually writes for the spiritual elite who must always provide leadership, periodically he declares what "the
people" should be told; and then he may sound utopian. Otherwise he tends to minimize the people by his theological distinc-
tions, for example when he remarks that it was not "religion"
that interfered with the advance of science—it was only "the anxiety and fanaticism" of some religious people. In particular his
ideal Protestantism at times seems Platonic or mythical; despite
his repeated allusions to the shortcomings of its churches, his
account of what Protestantism "really" means tends to obscure
what it has actually meant in history. I should never ask Tillich

to lower his spiritual sights, or to coddle the people, any more than the prophets of Israel or Christ did; but in assessing the religious situation of modern man I think we need to keep in mind the inescapable limitations of organized and popular religion, the invariable indignities that as Nicolas Berdyaev realized, are to some extent necessities. The risk and the courage required by faith as Tillich defines it must embrace the knowledge that most men are not yet clearly capable of such faith.

This is also to suggest, however, that religion is still a force to be reckoned with. Should the Communists succeed in dominating the world, they might conceivably manage to kill it, as some Christians fear; and I suppose it might be salutary for all Christians to realize that the survival of their religion is not guaranteed. Nevertheless, I doubt that the Communists could root it out, or would necessarily keep trying to do so. With success their fervor naturally tends to cool, they have a harder time keeping their followers keyed up, and they might even welcome some opium for their masses (just as sophisticates are now realizing that psychiatry may not be an adequate substitute for religion). The chief menace to religion, perhaps, is the possibility of something like Aldous Huxley's Brave New World, a mechanized society in which most men would fulfil the American dream of being well off and well adjusted, and life would be happy and hollow; but for most of the world there is very little prospect of such a comfortable state for a long time to come. This menace is largely confined to Christianity, in the affluent societies in the West. It brings up a question more immediately pertinent. Assuming that we manage to avoid catastrophe and maintain some kind of world order, what are the prospects of Christianity in the non-Western world?

Now, I take it that there is not the faintest likelihood of its

winning the world in the foreseeable future. Despite its thousands of missionaries, over the last century or so it has con-
verted only a minute fraction of the non-Christian peoples, has
had nothing like the success of Western science and technology,
or even of Western political ideals. It has made no inroads to
speak of on its major competitors, such as Mohammedanism and
Buddhism; so in view of the population explosion, Christians
will more likely become a still smaller minority. This prospect,
which is naturally disagreeable to the orthodox, may also distress
the many who believe that Christianity offers the clearest, deepest vision of the ideal unity of mankind—a very old dream that
has now become a more vivid hope, and to some extent a practical necessity.

Yet this ancient dream should remind us that all the higher
religions have preached the brotherhood of man. If the brotherhood is clearest in the Judaeo-Christian teaching of the father-
hood of God, orthodox Christians have most persistently obscured the ideal vision of unity by their dogmatism and exclu-
siveness. The conflicts that still prevent unity within Christianity itself have become a positive scandal in the lands it has been
trying to win, especially Africa, where in Uganda they led to
civil war between Catholic and Protestant missions. Christianity is further handicapped by its long association with Western
imperialism and colonialism, and the racial prejudice this fostered. Here Mohammedanism has an obvious advantage in its
traditional insistence on racial equality. Buddhism and Hinduism may have as great an advantage in their traditional tolerance,
and their offering of a kind of divine revelation that is perpet-
ually available to all men, implicit in their own nature, able to
make them spiritually self-sufficient.

In any case, it is by no means clearly desirable that there be one religion for our One World, or any total togetherness. Those in particular who cherish the ideals of a free society should welcome religious diversity, and might well fear any trend to uniformity in belief as much as the trends to standardization in culture and totalitarianism in political life. It is in the light of these secular ideals, indeed, that Christianity appears to best advantage and has most to offer the non-Western world.

Islam until lately made no effort to realize in political life the democratic principles of equality and fraternity stated in the Koran, and its liberals are still handicapped by its authoritarian tradition; few dare to say openly that Mohammed was a fallible mortal or that the Koran contains anything but the word of God. (Turks who aspire to a free society are therefore disturbed by the religious revival in their country, for this has been chiefly a resurgence of the old-time religion, with overtones of fanaticism.) Buddhism and Hinduism likewise inspired little social concern for the person, whose dignity was implicit in the exalted idea that the human soul is directly attuned to the World Soul, or is capable of completely transcending the world of sense and ego. Their tradition of "spiritual freedom" through unconcern with the temporal world, or the wisdom of non-attachment, might be the best kind of wisdom in a world threatened by catastrophe; but it does not encourage energetic efforts to avert catastrophe. Rather, it helps to account for the historic indifference of the holy men of India not only to the suffering of the masses but to such abominations as the caste of Untouchables, and today for the hostility to Hinduism of Nehru, as a leader seeking to further the earthly well-being of the priest-ridden masses.[1]

[1] Since the spokesmen of India are still given to boasting of its spirituality, and to a somewhat self-righteous impatience with the sins of the materialistic

Herein is perhaps the best argument for Tillich's devotion to the symbol of Christ on the cross. I see no possible way of proving that Christ is a "truer" symbol of the "really" ultimate than other religious prophets, or of disproving the teaching of Buddha, for instance, that life on earth is unworthy of ultimate concern. But one can argue that Christ is a more adequate or satisfying religious symbol for men who wish to take human history seriously, possibly the best symbol of at once the unmistakable tragedy of history and the spiritual values that man has nevertheless created and clung to, thereby achieving a measure of spiritual as well as material progress. And the fact remains that the Eastern societies are now developing something like the Western consciousness of history. While their wise and holy men may still say that time and history are unimportant, if not unreal, their national leaders are taking the temporal world quite seriously, as they must insofar as they seek to modernize their societies.

I still doubt that this effort will lead them either to the Christian faith, which is not essential to the adoption of modern science and technology, or to whatever kind of political state they aspire to. Those who assert that democracy can be maintained only on the basis of Christianity appear to forget not only that it was first established in ancient Greece without benefit of this faith, but that it will have to make its way in

---

West, it is fair to note that the land of sacred cows is still plagued by prejudice against the many millions of Untouchables, and that the most holy Brahmans are often reported to treat their servants most miserably. Even Arnold Toynbee—a great admirer of Indian spirituality—has remarked the common indifference to the spectacle of people dying of starvation in the streets, through which the sacred cows may wander. He added that the cows themselves may be allowed to starve—Hindus who would never kill them are not upset by their dying painfully.

the non-Western world on a different religious basis, perhaps even a secular one; else the efforts of Nehru and others are doomed. Meanwhile these efforts point instead to a possibly more ideal aspect of the actual religious drama on the world stage today. This is less a struggle among the higher religions for the loyalties of mankind, as in the bad old days of crusades and holy wars, than an increasing co-operation, mostly informal or unconcerted, but involving more consciousness of their common values, their common stakes in the world crisis, and of possible profit from their differences. The non-Western world is astir with Western ideals to which the Christian religion contributed; in recent years missionaries have participated ever more actively in technical assistance to the "backward" peoples, instead of trying first of all, as they used to, to get them to wear pants. On the other hand, Jung, Toynbee, Northrop, and others who have been extolling the values of the East, or its superior spiritual efficiency, have been underlining an influence of Eastern thought that has been active throughout our revolutionary era. (Ralph Waldo Emerson is among the early examples of it.) Still assuming that we manage to avoid catastrophe, one may speculate on the long-range possibilities of a higher synthesis of the higher religions: ideally, again, not a universal agreement on any one religious symbol or belief, but various efforts at reconciliation of differences, exploration of new religious possibilities, reflecting a deeper sense of the common interests of mankind, now brought together in One World. Or one may speculate (as Paul Tillich has) on further possibilities raised by the exploration of space, the discovery of different forms of life on other planets, perhaps even communication with other beings through electromagnetic signals: a possibility still remote but real enough to have started many men thinking, and perhaps salutary for Christian humility; for there might be forms of life higher than man, conceivably even beings who were not cursed by original sin, anyway affording some perspective on the brief history of man, the few thousand years in which he has been civilized, able to record his history on a relatively young, minor planet.

Unhappily, this recalls us to the terrible destructive power he has achieved, which makes all too conceivable the end of his history, makes it impossible to take for granted that he will have the wit not to blow up his world. In view of the current popularity of religion, I believe that we again need first to emphasize its shortcomings, or what Whitehead called the "dangerous delusion" that it is necessarily a good thing. Religion still works more obviously to divide than to unite mankind, in a One World that is still far from being a good neighborhood. Paul Tillich observes that "faith" confuses and misleads more often than not, and that today it is "more productive of disease than of health." It may thrive on other dangerous delusions. Jung himself paid religion a melancholy tribute when he demonstrated the abiding need of it, for he seemed pleased to point out that since Greek antiquity "the world has not been freed of one single superstition." The old-time religion indeed remains strong over most of the world, notably in India, Islam, and Latin America; but here it is not notably promoting the cause of either enlightenment or democracy. In the Christian world we can no more afford to count on religion as a pure spiritual tonic, much less as a cure for the moral and spiritual ills of men today.

Still, there is no denying the reality of these ills. They seem worse because of all the actual and potential goods coming out of modern science and technology, and they make it plainer that science and technology are only means to the good life, cannot for most men provide satisfying answers to the question of the meaning and purpose of their lives. Nehru, who on rational grounds is a severe critic of traditional religion, has also re-marked that for all its virtues rationalism is never enough, it does not penetrate to the "inner core" of man; and while he himself best illustrates the need for a broad conception of spirit-ual values, embracing more than the technically religious, he also points to the real spiritual needs that religion has satisfied throughout history, the lofty values it has created at its best. In attacking the dangerous delusion of its necessary goodness, Whitehead went on to say that the main point was its "tran-scendent importance" in human history. In our secular world it may seem less important; it has become a subject for scientific inquiry, or for cool historical analysis such as I have attempted here, while its great temples and cathedrals serve as tourist attractions; and today many if not most thoughtful believers would agree with Tillich that it cannot give us the immediate answers, cannot prophesy, cannot tell us anything certain about the end of our world. But I assume that ideally it still has much to offer, beyond consolation, in steadying men, nerving them, inspiring them to rise to the challenges of crisis. As one who also does not know the answers, I should point at the end to a broad protestant tradition in Christianity, reaching back to the proph-ets of Israel, which may be welcomed by skeptics too in the free societies. "The world will be saved, if it can be," wrote André Gide, "only by the unsubmissive"; and among the ambiguities of a religion that has preached a gospel of humility is that all along it has bred more of such proud, stubborn, troublesome types than has any other religion.

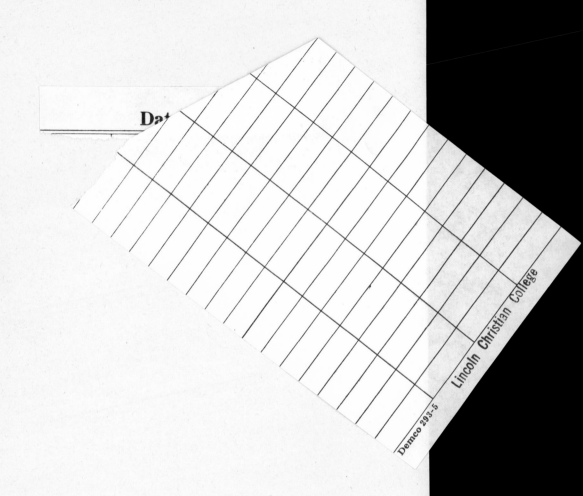